R.E. Smitley

GRACE IS NOT A BLUE-EYED BLOND

Grace

IS
NOT
A
BLUE
EYED
BLOND

R. Lofton Hudson

WORD BOOKS WACO, TEXAS

Grateful acknowledgment is made to the following for permission to use copyright material:
THE MACMILLAN COMPANY
GEOFFREY BLES, LTD.
    Quotations from *The New Testament in Modern English* by J. B. Phillips, copyright © 1958. Used by permission.
CAMBRIDGE UNIVERSITY PRESS
    Quotations from *The New English Bible, New Testament,* © The Delegates of the Oxford University Press and the Syndics of the Cambridge University Press, 1961. Used by permission.

Library of Congress Catalog Card Number: 68-21506
Printed in U.S.A.

PREFACE

The struggle of what to believe, how to apply our beliefs, and how to use disbelief wisely is going on in every person, religious or otherwise. We are in a day of paring down our traditions (reductionism), sometimes to the nub, in order to keep from being fools or from wasting time or words on meaningless concepts. We may have come to profess too little, but this will be simpler and more comfortable, perhaps more honest.

It has amazed me, as I have overcome the fear of being accused of heresy, how many good things I still see in religion and how much healthier I feel over being able to ignore intellectual bullies who would cram their particular brand of doctrine down my throat.

There is so much that I once believed that does not hold the slightest interest for me now. Life seems too short to quibble about God while we might be adventuring for Him— in personal response to Him, in relatedness to His creatures, and in trying to find His new word for our day.

This book is not intended to be a comprehensive survey of relevant Christian doctrines or of pertinent Christian ethics. It is but the way one believer sees some of the complex problems of trying to be a follower of Christ today.

This whole volume is addressed, in the title of next to the last chapter, to "Those Who Believe That They Believe." This is simply my way of saying that it is possible to believe without being opinionated. At least, I hope so.

R. Lofton Hudson

Kansas City, Missouri
February, 1968

CONTENTS

CHAPTER 1

Grace Is Not a Blue-Eyed Blond

A friend who goes to church occasionally was chatting with me rather casually about how little he knew about religion and how the religious terminology often puzzled him. I asked, "What do you think of when I say the word 'grace'?" His immediate reply was, "Why, Grace is a blue-eyed blond." I doubt that he could have done much better if he had been dead serious. If I had pressed him, he would have forced me to come to grips with my own religious jargon. And that might have been embarrassing.

Frequently, "grace" is used in a newspaper review to describe the free flowing movement of a ballet dancer and sometimes it is used to indicate the considerate and thoughtful attitude of one person in the presence of others. However, even though both uses have good denotations, other terms are fast replacing them. Besides, they have nothing of the ruggedness and significance which impregnated the religious terminology in the past and which so seldom finds a modern one-word counterpart to grace.

Grace is fast going out of use as a good, everyday word except by a sub-culture called the church. Imagine a fraternity man on the average college campus today saying as he leaves the frat house, "Okay, fellows, I'll represent the house in the talent contest, but if I win, it will be by the grace of God." Let's face it, they neither understand the meaning of grace nor do much business with God, and they wouldn't be caught dead spouting religious jargon.

Quite possibly, this distaste for religious language is due in part to the insipid manner in which "religious people" have talked about grace. And unfortunately, quite often very little grace may be found in those of us who call ourselves Christians. Then, too, it must be admitted that words do wear out, but strangely enough some words like "good," "bad," "truth," and "selfish" have lived.

What happened to the word *grace?* It was kept in the translations, even the modern speech ones, and is mouthed by Sunday school teachers and preachers "whose tones proclaim how flat and wearisome they feel their trade." (Coleridge).

Quite frankly, I believe that there is something in the experience symbolized by the word grace that is worth getting excited about. It is an experience, an interpersonal one, primarily (though being gracious to one's self is not extraneous to the Scriptures). It is not possible to define grace because it is always primarily a movement, an attitude, or a sentiment. And for these aspects of human living, we find illustrations, describe actions, and take moving pictures of them. But it is striking that we find no definition of grace in the Bible. However, we do find John the Apostle writing: "So the Word became flesh; he came to dwell among us, and we saw his glory, such glory as befits the Father's only Son, full of grace and truth . . . Out of his full store we have all received grace upon grace; for while the Law was given through Moses, grace and truth came through Jesus Christ" (John 1:14, 16-17, NEB).

It seems to me that these verses say that until the presence of Jesus in the world, religion consisted of rules, laws, commandments, duty, systems of conduct, knowing good and evil, and focusing upon good and evil as the way of pleasing God. When Jesus came, we saw one gracious act piled upon another (grace upon grace) as the ideal of life, and the gracious relationship became the primary fact of religion, rather than good and evil. The law had become an obsession, and obeying the law was a compulsion. Grace said that the law was not paramount, that freedom to respond to another person wholesomely and wholeheartedly is primary in religion. *Law* becomes a bondage; *grace* produces freedom— not the freedom to become enslaved by impulses, but the freedom to become our true selves in relationships with God and man.

Let me illustrate it by man-to-man relatedness. We should remember that any man-to-God relationship has to be similar to man-to-man reactions or it would be meaningless. For example, suppose life is discovered on Mars comprised of half man and half smoke. Quite obviously we cannot imagine what relationships with such a creature would be like. So, anthropomorphism or no anthropomorphism, we have to think of God's reactions to us as somewhat like those of another human being. Grace can be understood only within such a context.

Visualize, if you can, two human beings face to face with each other. In the usual categories they may be relating as parent-child, brother-sister, partners in business, chums, criminals in a gang, lovers, enemies, rivals, equals, superior-inferior, helper-needy, those who would hurt us, those who want to sit in our laps, those who for some reason find us repulsive, those who want to devour us. So you see, there are actually many different ways in which we relate to one another.

But, unfortunately, we tend to apply grace only to those who fit into certain categories of our making. We may find it quite easy to apply grace to people who are helpless and downtrodden; the stranger who may need a friend; the hunter who is lost in the mountains, or even someone who has offended us. But what about just any man—neighbor, relative, policeman, friend, member of the club—without reference to past events or status or "prior condition of servitude," or success? What keeps us from applying grace right across the board, like we do honesty, courtesy or fairplay? Is grace a word that is limited to only a few circumstances of life?

Let us look at two of the most common definitions of grace. "Grace is what everybody needs but nobody deserves." Grace is "unmerited favor." Both of these leave me cold. The word "deserves" and the word "unmerited" are loaded with the guilt-punishment approach to religion. The formula for such a religion reads something like this. "You are a bad person so I will punish you to make you better." An even worse formulation is: "Everybody who does a wrong deserves to be hurt so you are going to get hurt."

Personally, I resent such moralisms whether carried out in the name of God or in the name of Beelzebub. If done in the name of God, such punishments are indeed a violation of the Christian spirit. Recall the words of Jesus to James and John when they wanted to destroy a village in Samaria for not selling them food: "Ye know not what manner of spirit ye are of. For the Son of man is not come to destroy men's lives, but to save them" (Luke 9:55-56, KJV).

Quite possibly, concepts of grace that are smothered with ideas of law and justice may be of some help to those who conceive of God as vindicative and of human motivation as requiring threats and punishment, but there are certainly broader applications which apply to all cultures, all situations, and every event. If it applies only to a superior-inferior relationship as God-man or master-slave, it would not be a completely useless concept but it would imply prejudgment which does not become anyone except God. After all, who is inferior or sinful or slave?

You see, we are caught in the dilemma of playing God, dealt with by Paul in Romans One—the pagan who claimed to be wise—and in Romans Fourteen—the Christian who judged his fellow Christian—or that of an accepting relationship where man sees man in all of his limitations and refuses to judge.

Let us then examine the kind of relationships, or the kinds of relating, which are most frequent in our day-to-day patterns.

First, there is the benefactor-needy or dominant-passivity way of relating. This is the lot of the child. In a hundred different ways the child cries out, "Help me, please." To respond to this cry is not distinctly human. The parent beast or fowl responds, instinctively we say, to the needs of the young. Without this impulse, higher forms of life would not survive. But this is not grace. It is nature, if we may fall back on the ancient distinction between nature and grace (which I suspect of being invalid).

Then, there is the way of justice or duty. It is the way of

business, of contracts, of work. The word here is, "I will give you so much money for so much work." This area of life is one that has to be restructured and re-examined constantly because of the blindness and selfishness of man. It is the concern of both the church and the state.

This area of life constitutes the largest part of our existence. Our jobs, our reciprocal responses in our homes, our part of the community life, the payment of our honest debts, the willingness to work and to abide by just laws—these are the predominant parts of our lives. They are not grace any more than loving our natural children is grace. It is foolish to talk of going "the second mile" until we have gone the first. Grace is not in contrast with works or justice, it is beyond them. Knowing good and evil, which started "far away and long ago," somehow never saves man, it only enslaves him. Why? It must be for lack of grace.

At this point, it would seem to be of value (in addition to John's characterization of Jesus in John 1:14-17, quoted above), to see how the Bible uses the word "grace." Without attempting to delineate passages in the Old Testament, we may summarize by saying that both God and the saints of this Covenant are strange mixtures of will, impulse (devoid of justice), revenge, law, and graciousness. The Old Testament could not find a balance between the wrath of God and the love of God. There was a constant vascillation between law and love, with law and threats and punishments winning most of the time. In the Old Testament, we see God's face as frowning or fallen or turned away from even His own people. "He will not turn away his face *if*" is as far as the prophets ever got (e.g., II Chron. 30:9). The benedictory prayer that "the Lord make his face to shine upon thee" and "the Lord lift up his countenance upon thee" is still a prayer and, apparently, a long way from being realized yet in the thinking of religious mankind.

Modern Christians have not escaped the dilemma. One officer in the church who hears every sermon said to me in a counseling interview: "One Sunday I hear of the God who loves us and accepts us in spite of our faults and failures and who insists that we have that same attitude toward the homosexual, the criminal, and the Communist. The next I hear of a threatening God who says, 'Repent or perish,' and who will punish us if we do not tithe and attend church and firm up our attitudes against the Communists, the Nigger-haters, and the delinquents."

I know of a first grade school teacher who would draw a face that expressed anger if a pupil was naughty, and even have the pupil take the face home to the parent as a memento of his misbehavior. But if he had done well, she assumed that he would know enough to carry in his mind a picture of a shining or smiling face. Such a teacher would have made a great Old Testament prophet, or even a good legalist in certain modern Christian (?) situations. Her theme would read: "Be good or be frowned upon; be good or be rejected."

In contrast, the New Testament tries nobly to transcend such religious destructiveness. Paul summarized his own ministry as being devoted to "declaring the good news of the grace of God" (Acts 20:24 NEB). His own personal life movement he described in these words: "But by the grace of God I am what I am" (I Cor. 15:10). In both Corinthian letters and in his personal testimony to Timothy, he contrasts God's grace with the existential fact of his blasphemy and persecution of the church which he excuses by saying, "because I acted ignorantly in unbelief." The potent point is, however, that "the grace of our Lord overflowed for me with faith and love that are in Christ Jesus" (I Tim. 1:14).

A similar figure is used in Romans when Paul pictures the grace-faith response. "Through him (Christ) we have confidently entered into this new relationship of grace, and here we take our stand" (Rom. 5:2, Phillips). He describes this experience as the result of "the love of God flooding through our hearts by the Holy Spirit given to us" (Rom. 5:5, Phillips).

In a land thoroughly plagued with the scarcity of water, it is only natural that the image of flooding water should be used to describe the way God reacts toward us. Also, the wrath of God was often pictured as a flood, as being poured out on man. Visualize the dousing of a newly killed animal until the meat is clean and bright. Or the plentiful flow of cool clear water on a dirty and tired human body. Or even of a downpour of rain on parched earth and withering vegetables and crops. Or even of a cup spilling over with clear, cold water.

These figures are titillating, but precisely to what normal experience in human life do they refer? It is at this point that even great theologians, like Augustine, have fallen into error and talked of "infused grace." Some even speak of grace as a substance. And more popular teachers and preachers of religion speak of grace as if it were a Salk (polio) innoculation, or a heavenly oxygen tent in which we become securely encapsulated, or even as a perpetual magnanimous nipple to which we cling and from which we continuously draw in utter helplessness.

Not so. Grace is a term which has to do with the rich positive relationship between two people. A modern psychotherapist might describe it as a gracious confrontation in which one human being is secure and mature enough in himself to receive another without criticism, without preconceived notions of how the other ought to be, without judging, without impatience, and without any wish to make the other over into the therapist's image. And *with* some things too: with warmth, permissive acceptance of the other's uniqueness, with concern, with loyalty that respects the other's confidential communication, with openness to the other's revelation of himself, and with the therapist's willingness to reveal himself and how he sees the world, the self, and others. It is true that he sets limits on the interview such as time, rational behavior, and money compensations, but primarily the therapeutic relationship is a permissive and accepting and self-giving experience.

Listen now to a modern, Catholic, European theologian, Karl Rahner, as he talks of grace. "Grace is God himself, his communication, in which he gives himself to us as the *divinizing* loving kindness which is himself. Here his work is really himself, as the one communicated." He describes grace as "the natural openness to being as a whole," admits that "there is grace outside the church and her sacraments" and closes the chapter on "Nature and Grace" with the words: "Heart and grace are the only things which we cannot do without."[1]

It would seem, then, that grace is what happens between two persons. It is one giving himself to the other. It is responsibility toward another. It is a distinctive kind of relating. In a world of men turning their backs on one another, exploiting one another, trying to possess one another, killing

---

[1] Karl Rahner, *Nature and Grace* (Sneed and Ward, 1963), p. 24-25, 27, 44.

one another, gossiping about one another, and controlling one another, grace is one person confronting another in freedom and responsibility.

It is remarkable that modern man is trying to speak so clearly about how one person becomes present to another in a positive manner. Psychologists like Carl Rogers write extensively about empathy and acceptance. Psychiatrists like Paul Tournier (*Guilt and Grace*) speak of the "all-inclusive and unconditional love" as creating the environment for openness and confession. Peter Fransen, Catholic theologian, (in *Divine Grace and Man*) says in down-to-earth language that grace can never be a "thing possessed," nor something that hangs high above our heads like the aurora borealis on a frosty night; rather, God is like the sea, ebbing and flowing into each of us according to our needs and our accessibility. Each of these, and numerous other writers, are trying to speak to the deep felt needs of many of us.

Over fifty years ago John Oman, of Cambridge, England, was writing about "the gracious relationship" which God in Christ offers to man. He was trying to get us to see that faith was not submission to an omnipotent God whose mysterious emanations of power would get us sooner or later. Irresistible power does not provoke a true faith response. Yet, as Christ is usually presented, we have to see the lightning and the whirlwind before we can hear the still small voice. Too many preachers and teachers think they have to drag people through the hell of threats of punishment to get them to the heaven of favorable relationships.

Jesus, it seems, was different. In Him we saw grace upon grace, or a person full of grace and truth. Let us look at how He confronted man. All people are gracious to some and under some circumstances. Was He simply *some better?* Even the worst of people have amazingly good points, and the best appall us with their failures. How was Jesus different? Jesus was gracious to *all* men alike.

I am aware that as you read this you will be inclined to stand up and say, "But what about His driving the money changers out of the temple? And what about the names He called those conservative religious leaders of His day? (Cf. Matt. 23). Or what about that nasty remark He made to a Greek woman when she asked Him to cast out the demons from her daughter? (Cf. Mark 7:27 "It is not right to take the children's bread and throw it to the dogs.")

I must admit that I was shocked when I first read what He said to the Gentile woman. It seems, however, if we read this thoroughly that He was testing her faith. At least, when she got home the miracle of grace had been performed. And before condemning too strongly His words to the Pharisees, it would be helpful to have heard His tone of voice. Much may have been lost in the recording on paper.

Now, so far as the temple cleansing scene is concerned, I doubt that He lost His temper or experienced personal hate. Men have often been called upon to throw down idols and expell leaders of crime in order to pave the way for freedom and goodness. There must be some way to be gracious even in the face of needed revolution.

All one has to do to see the preponderance of evidence for the constant graciousness of Christ is to read the four Gospels. Peter summarized the reasons for believing Jesus to be the Son of God, in the house of Cornelius. He put gracious action, alongside the resurrection and at the heart of his arguments, as his reason for faith in Jesus' divinity. At one point he said that Jesus "went about doing good and healing all that were oppressed by the devil" (Acts 10:38).

Those who knew Jesus best, "beheld his glory." As Paul put it, they came to see "the light of the knowledge of the glory of God in the face of Christ" (II Cor. 4:6). What a striking statement!

Jesus confronted man at his worst and remained gracious.

I could mention the various examples of fallen women and tax-gatherers whom He lifted by His very manner. It would also be relevant to point out how He graced the home of Simon the Pharisee. It was grace that made Him stand in silence in the trial chamber and not strike back at His blatant accusers. And even greater grace that withheld criticism to "denying Peter" and "doubting Thomas."

There is a beautiful summary of Jesus' life by Carl Sandburg in "To a Contemporary Bunkshooter:"

> Jesus had a way of talking soft and outside of a few bankers and higher-ups among the con men of Jerusalem everybody liked to have this Jesus around because he never made any fake passes and everything he said went and he helped the sick and gave the people hope.
>
> This Jesus was good to look at, smelled good, listened good. He threw out something fresh and beautiful from the skin of his body and the touch of his hands wherever he passed along.[2]

Jesus would never have turned those rough and ready peasants of Palestine into pioneering missionaries if He had not been able to manifest a drastic grace. No cheap grace, to use Bonhoeffer's word, would have done what Jesus did.

---

[2]From "To a Contemporary Bunkshooter" from *Chicago Poems* by Carl Sandburg. Copyright 1916 by Holt, Reinhart and Winston, Inc. Copyright 1944 by Carl Sandburg. Reprinted by permission of Holt, Reinhart and Winston.

He met them at their worst and entered into their tragedies. I know of a psychotherapist who spent two years patiently listening to a patient's stories and escapades without getting visible results. In desperation one day the therapist burst into sobs saying, "I have done all I know to do; I have failed; you are exactly as you were when you came to me." In utter amazement the patient left the office. It was incredible that anyone could care that much about whether or not she got well. From that day the patient showed improvement. Later she said, "All my life I have thought that I did not matter to anyone so I did not care whether I changed or not."

In religion we would say that the therapist's behavior was redemptive. Whatever we call it, grace had become profoundly expressed. It would have been easier to blame the patient, or to dismiss her as just one of those who was "not motivated for therapy."

To use another example, the Apostle Paul confronted Jesus with a situation that to him was intolerable. It was some kind of "thorn in the flesh"—something that was constant and painful and should be removed it seemed. The Divine reply was: "My grace is sufficient for you, for my power is made perfect in weakness" (II Cor. 12:9). Whether Paul was plagued by a physical disease like epilepsy or glaucoma, a social situation like unfair criticism, a tantalizing temptation, or just spiritual lethargy, it was the grace to grin and bear it that was given. Grace finds many ways to confront the human situations, no one of which need be known ahead of the event that calls for grace.

There are many other things which could be said about the applications of grace. It is by grace that we are saved, through faith (Eph. 2:8). It is the gift of God. Communication is always a gift. Meeting another in terms of his needs is a gift. To exceed the other's need by our "abounding grace" (Rom. 5:20) is the act of God, and it is the responsibility of the Christian.

Primarily, grace is a face, the face of Christ and of Christian acceptance. All of us are familiar with the non-verbal communication of faces. Some very polite faces mask indifference or fear or downright hate. Some frank, open faces invite us to be our unique selves and to rise higher toward our goals of wholeness and happiness. Some faces scream (without an audible word) criticism, or rejection, or threats.

Dr. Karl Menninger in his book, *The Vital Balance,* is discussing at one point the negativistic personality which at first says "no" to almost everything. These "troubled patients," as he calls them, have never made an unsound loan, or voted for a liberal cause, or sponsored any extravagances. They cannot permit themselves the pleasure of giving. He describes them as "rigid, chronically unhappy individuals, bitter, insecure, and often suicidal."

In illustrating the contrast between the positive and negative attitudes toward life he tells the story about President Thomas Jefferson and a group of companions, riding horseback cross-country, and were obliged to ford a swollen stream. A wayfarer waited until several of the party had crossed and then hailed President Jefferson and asked to be ferried across. The President took him up on the back of the horse and later set him down on the opposite bank. "Tell me," asked one of the men, "why did you select the President to ask this favor of?" The man answered, "I didn't know he was the President. All I know is that on some of the faces is written the answer 'no' and on some of them the answer 'yes.' His was a 'yes' face."[3]

It seems to me that the Bible is trying to tell us that grace means that God has a "yes" face. He receives us and continues to keep this countenance. And that this is the face that we Christians are supposed to present to the world.

I should like to close with reference to an idea presented by the late French writer, Albert Camus. In *The Rebel,* a tremendous study of modern times and man's revolt against the past, Albert Camus says that only two possible worlds can exist for the human mind "the sacred (or, to speak in Christian terms, the world of grace) and the world of rebellion." Near the end of this book, he remarks that in the nineteenth century, with Nietzsche, Marx, and others, the struggle was one of justice against grace and truth. In fact, he goes so far as to say that the nineteenth century was dominated by the question of "how to live without grace." Even more striking is his further remark that in the twentieth century the question which tortures the contemporary world is: "how to live without grace and justice."[4]

We cannot help but hope that by the twenty-first century we may be far enough along in our quest for the richer life together and in our rebellion against injustice, that grace—in the deep, profound, and thoroughly Christian sense—may be the dominant theme of our world. It is possible that we will never see the twenty-first century unless we come to know the true meaning of grace, and practice it.

---

[3]Karl Menninger, M.D., with Martin Mayman, Ph.D. and Paul Pruyser, Ph.D., *The Vital Balance* (New York: The Viking Press, 1963), pp. 204-205.
[4]Albert Camus, *The Rebel* (New York: Alfred A. Knopf, Inc., Vintage Books, 1956), pp. 21, 225.

CHAPTER 2

The Big Sins of Little Sinners

An evangelist is reported to have announced that there are five hundred and seventy-seven different sins that people commit. He received thousands of letters from people who wanted the list—possibly they were afraid they had missed some.

Quite likely you have noticed that hardly anyone admits to being either free from sin or as being a sinner. We neither claim to be perfect—or even care to, most of us—nor do we admit that there is much wrong with us. We may be a little sick, a trifle criminal, somewhat cranky or crabbed, "incurably religious but not much," and even violators of the law on certain occasions and under certain circumstances. But to want to be perfect is to be square right out of Squaresville. We are all *little* sinners in our own eyes. Pascal wrote two striking things about the way people see themselves: "What astonishes me most is to see that all the world is not astonished at its own weaknesses." And: "There are only two kinds of men: the righteous who believe themselves sinners; the rest, sinners, who believe themselves righteous."

We are like the man who was reprimanded by the preacher for cussing. He said, "Oh, preacher, you know how it is; you pray a little and I cuss a little but neither of us means anything much by it."

I think the best definition of sin in the Bible is found in James 4:7: "Whoever knows what is right to do and fails to do it, for him it is sin." It lifts sin out of the guilt producing, negative, condemnation frame of reference and puts it in the challenge, call, constructive, creative category. But, unfortunately, most people do not distinguish between sin, crime, taboo, wrong, and sickness. *Crime* is the violation of a law. Usually law violation is a sin, but not always—as in the case of the American colonists in refusing to pay taxes without representation in the British Parliament. *Taboo* is a restriction against something, like the eating of pork by a Jew, but it may not necessarily be a sin. I asked a Christian Jew once if he really thought that a person who ate pork could get to heaven. He replied, "Yes; in fact, the more pork he eats the quicker he will get there."

Wrong is a different category still. It is based on custom or societal requirements. It may be wrong to walk on the grass in the park or to use two parking spaces, but, certainly these would not be considered sins.

Then there is *sickness*, which is often confused with sin. For example, the alcoholic is sick. Although earlier in his drinking career, when he could still quit and didn't, he was sinning. The kleptomaniac, one who steals compulsively, is sick. He may also be sinning in other aspects of his living, but he has little control over some kinds of stealing. It controls him.

Sin is, strictly speaking, a religious concept, a theological dogma. Often it is used in a very childish manner to mean what is socially or religiously disapproved—it is sin to cuss or smoke or steal or fish on Sunday. In this usage, to say, "It is a sin," usually means that "I condemn what you are doing because I don't like to do it, or I am too old or too scared to try it." It is interesting to note that people tend to condemn the sins in others that they are not at present committing, or which they are committing under cover and feel guilty about, or wish to commit and feel a sly envy of those who do these sins.

Alexander Pope wrote:

> Vice is a monster of so frightful mien,
> As to be hated needs but to be seen;
> Yet, seen too often, familiar with her face,
> We first endure, then pity, then embrace.

Essay on Man, Epistle II 1. 217

I do not believe this. Sin or vice is so desirable that it comes to us in the armor of a savior, with the fragrance of a seductress, and in the role of liberator from every ill which we suffer, especially boredom. No, sin is no monster, but a missioner sent to call us to a supposedly fuller life.

Look at how differently Jesus approached this whole problem of sin. To Him, sin was a breach of fellowship, a turning of good talent into bad channels, a failure to become—an attempt to be somebody that we aren't, such as trying to be God, or an attempt to play God.

Four of His own illustrations portray His understanding of sin—all found in the Gospel of Luke.

The Good Samaritan story (chapter 10) is about two very religious people traveling to a convention down at Jericho.

Finding a man beaten by a robber beside the road half dead, they looked but decided to go ahead to the meeting and talk about brotherly love instead of doing anything about it. The Samaritan, though a half-breed, put himself out for the wounded man, thus saving the lives both of himself (spiritually) and the robber (physically). He "was moved with pity" (Luke 10:33 NEB). He saw himself in his suffering neighbor.

Then, in Chapter 12, there is the farmer who had a bumper crop, built new barns, decided to live in luxury and ease and merriment and to hell with the rest of the human race. "So is he who lays up treasure for himself, and is not rich towards God" (Luke 12:21).

The story of the Prodigal Son and of the Elder Brother is well-known. The son who is the villian turns a hero. The elder brother, as conforming as an IBM computer, turns out to be as hollow as a silo and as petty as a spoiled child.

The fourth story is found in Luke 18. Two people went to church, or synagogue. One felt good because he had not violated the community mores and he had lived up to the religious ideals of private devotions and of tithing his income. Also, and incidentally, he looked down his nose at people who were guilty of impulse, spontaniety, and opportunism.

The other, an internal revenuer, had nothing to commend himself for except that he was hated and regretted it. "God, be merciful to me a sinner" probably meant, "I want to belong and I know that I have to change to do so." Jesus caught his spirit and cleansed him from past failures and stupidities. He did it because He saw that the man was open to change and was not committed to perpetuating his past errors. What an opportunity this was for the Master!

These four stories are little "movie shorts," catching people in the act of living in sin. But to be perfectly honest, sin is never accurately defined. Sin is illustrated. It is a state, a condition, a negative relationship to God and man. These four stories portray people going along through life assuming that all is well with them but actually "living behind God's back." They were guilty of big sins but they all considered themselves little sinners. We can classify their sins—colossal in God's eyes but miniature in their own—under three categories.

First, there was the sin of *denial of indebtedness*. Most every Sunday, and sometimes in between, we say, "Forgive us our debts as we forgive our debtors." The Apostle Paul said in one of his letters: "I am debtor both to the Greeks and to the Barbarians; both to the wise and to the unwise" (Rom. 1:14).

It is a little recognized fact that every person is in debt. We never get out of debt. The only people who are paid up are in cemeteries. To live is to be indebted—to God and to man. Sleep is merely a brief, daily moratorium on our indebtedness. This does not mean that we have to live constantly under the strain of creditors pressing us. It is not necessary to become addicts of the strenuous life. Rather, calmly and confidently we need to commit ourselves to the fact that what we are, have, can acquire, or can become is not ours to use as we wish. We owe it. To be a human being is to be in debt.

The selfmade man who worships his creator is an example of what I am talking about. Such a man, I believe, is suffering from a delusion. We owe to history, to society, if not to God, all that we are and all that we can become.

The Prodigal Son said, "Give me the share of the property that falls to me." The rich farmer said "I" or "my" eleven times in discussing with himself what he would do with his affluent circumstances. Then, as if he were sick of himself, he began addressing his soul as "you." When a man denies his indebtedness, he becomes alienated from himself (his soul) and talks to himself as he would to another, a comparative stranger.

In the Good Samaritan story the robber represents a radical viewpoint stated in a formula: "What is yours is mine if I can get it." The priest and Levite would have said: "Mine is mine and I will keep it if I wish." The Samaritan operated on the principle: "What is mine is yours if you need it more than I do." "Go and do likewise."

The Pharisee (in Luke 18) not only denied his indebtedness to God or man, he held himself higher than both.

Carl R. Rogers, noted psychologist, has said that two beliefs are back of most of the serious tension situations that arise between individuals, groups, or nations. They are: I am right and you are wrong; and I am good and you are bad.

Jesus' story of the way this Pharisee prayed illustrates these two formulations perfectly. "God," he was saying, "don't you dare question my standing before you for I am right. Look by way of contrast at this tax collector. I am good, by way of contrast with him and others. I do not owe anything. I have payed my debt by doing what I was supposed to do."

Walter Winchell quoted a poem by A. T. Lanta, entitled "Saints Who Have Never Been Caught." In the first two stanzas the poet complains bitterly of the gossip and harsh criticism and unfair judgments of such people. In the closing stanza he says:

I'm a sinner O Lord, and I know it . . . I'm weak, I blunder,
I fail . . .
I'm tossed on life's stormy ocean; like ships embroiled in a
gale.
I'm willing to trust in Thy mercy; to keep the commandments
Thou'st taught . . .
But, deliver me, Lord, from the judgment . . . of Saints who
have never been caught.

"Everyone who exalts himself will be humbled, but he who humbles himself will be exalted" (Luke 18:14).

"My life is mine; I will do with it as I please." "I am not hurting anyone but myself." "If I want to drink myself to death, it is nobody else's business." These and other assumptions about who we are and how we are related to people are back of most of our sins. The big sin is denial of indebtedness.

A second mammoth sin is *unpotentiality*. Most concepts can be broken down into simple five cent, Anglo-Saxon words. This one is more difficult. "Becoming" is not the same as reaching our potentiality. "Growth" is a process term without a goal in mind, usually.

Unpotentiality means that we are not fulfilling ourselves, not unfolding, not becoming who we were created to become. If this sounds too idealistic or absolutistic, I am being misunderstood. I have no exact knowledge of what you or I could be before we expire. Perhaps we shall even fulfill ourselves in the next world. But the sin lies in not unfolding, like the lily, in not moving toward our goals. When our patterns of life are frozen, our achievements have too low ceilings and our personal expansions meet hard crusts of hopelessness or lack of ambition, we perish.

The late Harry Stack Sullivan, pioneer psychiatrist, said, "Most people are caricatures of the persons they might have been."

Erick Fromm wrote in *Man for Himself:*

> It is part of the tragedy of the human situation that the development of self is never completed; even under the best conditions only part of man's potentialities is realized. Man always dies before he is fully born.[1]

How like the New Testament this sounds! "Ye must be born again,"—start all over and allow God to release or implant new forces, to make a new creature who never stops becoming. "Except ye be converted and become as little children"—not settled down to the commonplace and the stereotyped. "What does it profit a man if he gains the whole world and loses or forfeits himself?" (Luke 9:25).

Anyone who stops growing as a person, who does not move steadily toward his potential, might be like a school boy who plays hookey every day of spring and then wonders why he fails to get his diploma. Our fate is partly in our own hands—largely in fact—and we must decide what we become as well as what we may achieve. It is not always possible to know what will become of us, but we can determine what we will become while living these few years upon this earth.

The priest and Levite failed to reach their potential, in the Good Samaritan story, by not seizing the moment of opportunity. The rich farmer was born a human being and died a land owner. The Prodigal Son got off on the wrong

---

[1] Eric Fromm, *Man For Himself* (New York: Holt, Rinehart and Winston, Inc.), p. 91.

track but soon retraced his steps. The elder brother stayed on the right track but never went forward as a perceptive human being. The Pharisee stagnated like a pool of water, rotting by the natural process of self-admiration. The tax collector "flowed out on new plains" not knowing where his confession would lead him.

This brings us to a natural climax of sins. Back of denial of indebtedness and of unpotentiality is the very basic problem of *closedness*.

Let me explain it this way. A little child is open and frank and undefensive. He says what he feels and is trusting toward others to the point of gullibility. At the other end of a long continuum is the silent schizophrenic patient sitting on the floor, crouched down in a fetal position, not speaking to anyone or paying any attention to anyone else on this mental hospital ward. He is *closed* for the time being.

Between these two, the open child and the closed mental patient, are all the rest of us. From the time we told our first lie and got by with it, we have known that we could close up to those about us and keep our secrets—secret sins and secret joys. All of us are daily in the process of opening and closing. If we close too much, people say that they do not know us, that we are introverts. We find, however, that closing is a protective device. Like the tortoise, we close when we imagine danger.

But a man is a Christian precisely depending on his openness to God and to man. Not to be open to God in prayer and honest praise is a kind of prideful unbelief. To be closed to man, especially to those in need, is to be closed to Christ. Not to be open to the future, to the leadership of the Holy Spirit, to accept what comes, is a kind of resistance to God, or even outright defiance.

I have counseled with many people who were complaining of depression and sadness. Some of these, not all, were depressed because they were guilty. They were not guilty of drunkenness or stealing or adultery, but they were guilty of sitting down beside the road of life and just observing—refusing to get involved. So many people today are closed up to the vital issues and the filthy problems around them—closed to life. How tragic that so many of us are encapsulated in our hates, our fears, our indifference, and our small ideas.

In the four stories that we are considering, the Samaritan "as he journeyed"—the key phrase in the whole passage—was open to the needs of the people about him. The priest and the Levite were preoccupied with the overall picture of things. The Samaritan lived in the moment. The others were thinking only of Jericho.

The rich farmer was open to *things*, not to people. When he talked to himself, he spoke to his soul almost as if he were addressing a machine. He had no vertical and few horizontal connections. He lived on an "I-it" existence, not "I-you."

The Prodigal Son, like every adolescent, tried to withdraw from family relations. His experiment in "loose living" landed him in the pig pen. But "he came to himself" and realized that he was a creature of relationships. He woke up, then he rose up. Soon he was seeking relatedness. His older brother had stayed at home; he was there but never *all* there. No wonder it says so dramatically and simply, "He was angry and refused to go in" to the feast. Some people stay outside of life and never go in. Sulking is death to society.

Let's take a final look at the Pharisee and the tax collector. Both of them began their prayers by addressing God. The Pharisee's prayer was five times as long as the tax collector's. Both used the personal pronouns—I, me. Wherein lay the difference? One was open to God and man—the words, "a sinner," could be nothing else but a cry for relatedness and an admission of irresponsibility. The other, the Pharisee, said a prayer but he did not pray. He never responded to God as God. And he could not relate to other sinners as being like himself.

Through the ages men have prayed both kinds of prayers, those of arrogance and those of humility. Only as men have knelt, have their statures become very much the same. Looking down almost closes the eyes. When we meet eye-ball to eye-ball we see ourselves in our neighbors' eyes. Closedness becomes a sin, closely akin to death, because man's true state is openness.

> Sitting still may be to sin.
> Shutting my mouth may be to scold.
> Mouldy thoughts decay within;
> Flaccid muscles, not old, turn cold.
> Despair and fear, twins to hate,
> Go hiding under the bed of love.
> There stay hid until too late;
> Then we blame our stars above.
>   R. L. HUDSON

CHAPTER 3

The Handicap of Our Pretenses

I suspect any man who denies that he is a hypocrite. Of course, this calls for a definition of hypocrisy. We probably think it is merely pretending to be something that we are not. That is the usual definition. But even by that definition we are deceitful. We are such divided selves and such split personalities that most of us really do not know who we are and what we feel at a particular time.

Milton said, quite accurately, it seems to me:

> Neither man nor angel can discern
> Hypocrisy, the only evil that walks
> Invisible, except to God alone.

Why are we so prone to call people hypocrites? What did Jesus mean by calling people hypocrites? Is this not just another way of using labels to keep from having to think? Is not the word "hypocrite" a club used to clobber people we don't like? On the other hand, what is the social and religious reality which we confront when we cry, "Hypocrite?"

Any serious student of Jesus Christ would have to admit He was the mortal enemy of sham, cant, pretense, braggadocio, and strut. Phonies were not funny to Him. They were damaged souls, deformed minds turning goodness and religion into selfish ends. Most of us remember His telling the disciples not to be like the hypocrites who love to pray in public to be seen of men; and that they gave alms to the poor when people would see and praise them. And on another occasion He issued a sharp rebuke about judging others. "You hypocrites, first take the log out of your own eye, and then you will see clearly to take the speck out of your brother's eye" (Matt. 7:5, RSV).

What does hypocrisy mean? We can only understand this if we get down to the bedrock of our understanding of ourselves and see that every person consists of a mask, or front, or facade, which we show to others, and also the real self which God (as Milton said) sees.

The outward pattern, the mask (*persona*, from which we get our word "personality") is symbolically presented in the Genesis story by clothes. "Then the eyes of them both were opened, and they knew that they were naked; and they sewed fig leaves together and made themselves aprons" (Gen. 3:7, RSV). A little farther on it says, "Unto Adam also and to his wife did the Lord God make coats of skins, and clothed them" (Gen. 3:21). It is extremely superficial, if not ridiculous, in the light of man's social history, to think that this making of clothes had anything to do with modesty or being ashamed for their bodies to be seen. Why should they not have covered their faces also, if this were true, and peep out at each other through tiny slits?

No, the Bible is trying to tell us that as soon as we become aware of ourselves as being "relaters" in relationships, we become self-conscious. This has nothing to do with sex or morality in the usual sense of the word. It does concern the fact that every human being *prepares a face* every time he confronts another human being. Another way of saying the same is that the clothes we wear, our gestures, our very outward manner are necessary to living, to dealing with interpersonal relationships.

The fact that God made them clothes is simply saying that all of us consist of the front we put up to the world and the self we look in at when we pause. No man ever escaped this duality or splitness in personality. It is the way we are by God's creation.

Nietzsche says that "every profound mind needs a mask." Emmanuel Kant in his *Anthropology* says that anyone who fails to grasp the significance of the false appearances in the world, and who opposes them, is a traitor to humanity.

This brings us to the crux of the problem of hypocrisy. All of us wear masks—they may even vary from day to day. Some mornings I am all smiles, and really feel smiley inside; on others I am as closed as a clam and wear a poker face. People may appear to be bad when actually they are good. The issue of a *hindering hypocrisy* arises when either I cease trying to be honest with myself, or I put on a big front and intend to deceive others for selfish gains.

Only God can deal with the second form of hypocrisy. In our blindness to our mixed motives we can hardly peel off the hypocritical layers enough to know why we behave as we do. And we certainly are at loss in judging our fellow man.

Sometimes a psychotherapist may help an individual to peer behind his screen of rationalizations and see his true motives. I remember telling a counselee of mine that if she made progress in coming to know herself, it would probably be extremely painful at points. A year later, after regular weekly visits, she said: "You told me that it would be painful, but I had no idea how painful it would be to look at myself. I've been filled with hate all my life and didn't realize it."

The fact is that the most commonly recognized form of pretense of hypocrisy is in claiming to be better than we are. All of us want to be liked by someone, if by no one except our dog. Most of us want the respect and admiration of many. And some of us go to great pains to get into a position of being worshiped. The normal need to appear well in the eyes of others becomes frustrated, because we find it so hard to be good people, and we choose the alternative of "acting." Martin Buber paid his respect to this problem in his last book (*The Knowledge of Man*) as he discusses "being and seeming" as two different types of existence, the latter referring to people who are overconcerned with the effect they are producing in the other person.

Matthew 23 is filled with examples of this spurious goodness. Some of the most graphic things Jesus ever said are contained here. He likened their lives to cups washed on the outside but filthy inside, or to tombs whitewashed on the outside but full of decaying bodies within.

It seems to me, however, that religious people ought to assume a part of the responsibility for setting the stage for this kind of hypocrisy. We cause people to be hypocrites. Not only religious people, but the whole society does. We honor the good person instead of merely praising the good deed. We are so activist oriented that people cannot respect and love themselves unless they are producing. It seems to me that we leave people with the impression that unless they live up to our standards we will gossip about them or punish them in some other way. Such attitudes lead people to doing little show-off deeds of measurable and reportable goodness while neglecting "the weightier matters of the law, judgment, mercy, and faith" (Matt. 23:23).

Not only by doing little things and neglecting the big ones do we become hypocritical, but we often substitute talking for doing. "He talks a good game" we hear someone say in derision or humor.

The fact is, the human mind is so constructed that an idea can become almost synonymous with a deed. We imagine ourselves doing something and may feel almost as satisfied as if we had done it. We may say to the clerk in the store "I'm just looking, thank you," but that will not get our shopping done.

The psychotic (insane) person may lose all distinction between idea and act and think that he has really murdered someone because he thought of it. Likewise, a fairly sound-minded person may think "I believe in God and take an interest in Christ's work; I read the church paper and the religious section of the Saturday newspaper; I must be deeply religious." To paraphrase a verse from the Letter of James: "Be one who carries out your religious practices, not a reader about or hearer of religious ideas" (Jas. 1:22, Phillips).

Besides doing little easy things in life, and substituting talking for doing, many people get to thinking they are better than they are because of what they used to do. "Leaning back on your laurels" would be a good name for this. Just as the road to hell is paved with good intentions, so the road to stagnation and spiritual failure is paved with pleasant memories of what we have done. This is not to say that we should not enjoy our memories of past accomplishments, but they hardly make a good substitute for becoming what we can become. Few things are more pathetic than to see middle-aged or elderly people fingering over past memories when new productions are waiting to be turned out. One thing I suppose is worse, to rehearse all the bad things that ever happened to you—absolutely no one would want to hear that, not even your psychiatrist.

The gist of what I am saying is that by majoring on minors, by talking instead of acting, and by thinking back instead of looking forward we often fall into the error of feeling that we are better than we are. From this feeling, recurring often enough, we move into a kind of hypocritical stance, a manner, a pose, and even a strut. It might be called "the saint complex" or "the halo syndrome." The truth is, to-day, however, there are few people who would want to be called saintly, but there are a good many people who carry about an air of don't-accuse-me-of-anything.

Such must have been the impression given by the woman sitting in the church pew in front of Robert Burns. He noticed the haughty way she held her head and the light touch of her fingers against her hair. Then, to his amusement and amazement, he saw a louse crawl out from under her hat. That was supposed to have been the inspiration for Burns' poem, "To a Louse" in which he said:

> O wad some Pow'r the giftie gie us
> To see oursels as ithers see us!
> It wad frae monie a blunder free us . . .

But there is another kind of hypocrisy which is probably more widespread—the middle aged and elderly profess too much, youth too little. I refer to the kind of hypocrisy that pretends to be wild, lewd, unbelieving, completely unconcerned, and certainly uncommitted. I find young people confessing to me rather sheepishly sometimes, that they do try to pray, and that they really do not think all of the bad thoughts which their parents credit to them. You would think by hearing them argue, however, that the world in the next generation is certainly to be not a utopia but a sociopathic slum.

What does such negative hypocrisy mean?

It actually means many things. Some are rebels without a cause and really are looking for something to make their lives distinctive. Others are merely drawing attention to themselves. The hypocrite is always both the archer and the target, aiming really at his own self-adulation. Still others are those who know inherently that conformity may be a vice and are trying to prove their own right and power to stand their full heights and not bow down to the past. They refuse to be a set of obsolete responses but in their loud protests they are professing a new absolute—that only the new is true.

These pretenders of novelty call to mind one of Luke's descriptions of the Athenians in Paul's day who "spent their time in nothing except telling or hearing something new" (Acts 17:21). They believe that the mind must be like a parachute in use, always open. They have forgotten that the mind can be like the mouth, open to receive, but it needs ultimately to be closed on something.

It seems to me that there is a modern version of hypocrisy which professes to be more irreligious than it really is—incurably religious but *not much* may be the best description; looking worse in the eyes of society than it really is; with newer and fewer values than it is expected to profess; and freer than any generation which has ever lived. They pretend to be way out!

Oscar Wilde characterizes these negative hypocrites in *The Importance of Being Earnest:*

> I hope you have not been leading a double life, pretending to be wicked and being really good all the time. That would be hypocrisy.

An example of such hypocrites are the modern doubters. They say, with Nietzsche, "God is dead." The enlightened religionist says, "Sure, we have known that *that* God you are talking about was dying for fifty years; now, in the name of Christ let's give him a decent funeral." The doubter says, "But I refuse blind faith; I cannot believe the Christian dogmas." "So what?" the theologian answers, "If you cannot give intellectual assent to statements of doctrine, try looking at Christ; He may come alive; if He does you will meet God." "But you do not understand. I doubt that there is a God," the new hypocrite says. "Good" says the theologian. "I do, too. He does not exist like the tree exists. He is not in the world; the world is in Him. Now which will you live by, your faith or your doubt? In every heart faith and doubt sit side by side. I choose to live by my faith, though pared down some by my reason."

I do not ask anyone to profess to be better than or believe more than he can find it in his heart to do so. Even Christ respected the doubt of Thomas. And to two disciples who were open minded and inquiring, Andrew and Simon Peter, he said, "Come and see" (John 1:39). They saw and then they believed. I doubt that Jesus even felt good about blind faith. Pretense will often preclude faith.

Tennyson was right:

There lives more faith in honest doubt,
Believe me, than in half the creeds.
In Memoriam

Let us turn now to a third and final form of hypocrisy or
pretense that underlies the other two—we pretend to be
stronger than we are—our real disgrace is to show weakness—
we must be strong. This may be, in the religious sense, a kind
of spiritual gigantism. Or in the emotional sense—we are not
in danger of alcoholism or nervous breakdowns like our
neighbors. Or concerning our marriages; others may fail, but
divorce is out of the question for me and my house. Or under
no circumstances must we show fear, even in the face of our
own or our friend's death.

One night I sat in the hospital with a friend. Over a period
of years I had seen her through several serious illnesses in
that very hospital. Now she said: "Dr. Hudson, this time I
am not going to make it." What does one say in a time like
this? "Don't worry about it; there is a better place to live
which you have never visited." "We all have to die some-
time." "Don't talk like that; you have pulled through other
serious illnesses; you may make this one." I could have
quoted her John Donne's "Death, be not proud, though
some have called thee Mighty and dreadful, for thou art not
so . . . Death, thou shalt die!" But she did not need a literary
recitation at this time. She was weak, in body and spirit, and
admitted it. My simple reply, which I had never made to
anyone before or since, was this, "None of us is." I felt it to
the soles of my feet, and I stood stripped of my hypocrisy.
I was speaking as a dying man to a dying woman.

Or take the case of a very strong woman who called me
one night at 9:30 and reported that her husband had fallen
dead of a heart attack and was being taken to the funeral

home. Her generous words were, "Now, Pastor, you needn't come out to the house; my son is here and I am making it fine." I begged to be allowed to come to her side for a few minutes at least, and she consented. Most people, I suppose, would have thought her very brave and strong. She hardly shed a tear even though she and her husband had shared in a wonderful relationship. I did not understand it and cautioned her not to try to be too strong. The doctor sent her some medicine but it did not take effect until early the next morning. Then the break came. She quietly went into a state of shock which lasted for three days, and she missed the funeral entirely.

I could not help but wonder if the church had not taught her not to grieve—forgetting to enlarge upon the words, "as others who have no hope" (1 Thess. 4:13). It is possible that she might have recovered much more quickly if she had surrendered to her normal feelings.

I feel terribly weak when I try to understand why people have such a need to be strong. Of course, we need to grow and manage ourselves as maturely as possible in trying circumstances. Falling down and wallowing in the gutters of our failures, or of life's mishaps, is certainly no occasion for a blue ribbon. There are times, we all know, when we need to "screw our courage to the sticking point," put one foot in front of the other, and hold ourselves together until the cyclone passes. But why in heaven's name do we think we have to be Goliaths, or Samsons, or Atlases, or Achilles, or Beowulfs?

Let me face for myself and with you the following situations: How would you take it if you were in prison for life? Have you ever imagined how it would feel to be a homosexual?—or, terribly shaky and afraid of having to spend the rest of your life in a mental hospital? What would death look like if you were to face it eyeball to eyeball, to use a modern expression? How would it feel to have a slow-moving but incurable disease?

A friend of mine who was a theological professor (and to my way of thinking, a very sound Christian), lost his only child, a very brilliant fourteen-year-old son. Years later he told me, "You cannot imagine how close I came to becoming an atheist. I doubted immortality. I couldn't make sense out of anything. It took me months to get my bearings."

No, none of us is strong. We are weak. We "suffer the slings and arrows of outrageous fortune" with reluctance and puzzlement, and sometimes horror. The trouble, it seems to me, is not merely a lack of faith but a surplus of pretense. We have an image of ourselves which accumulates from infancy on and then we fall for it. This is especially true of the person who rises above the crowd, either as a Christian or a secular leader.

Dag Hammarskjold in his *Markings* wrote:

> Around a man who has been pushed into the limelight, a legend begins to grow as it does around a dead man. But a dead man is in no danger of yielding to the temptation to nourish his legend, or accept its picture as reality. I pity the man who falls in love with his image as it is drawn by public opinion during the honeymoon of publicity.[1]

The kind of pretense or hypocrisy which cripples, hinders, encapsulates, and stops real growth is that where individuals develop a pride system and images of what they *ought* to be (converted into what they pretend they are already)—from

[1]Dag Hammarskjold, *Markings,* (New York City, Alfred A. Knopf, 1964), p. 66.

there, the process moves from putting on one armour after another, anything to keep from seeing the truth about themselves.

In reading the Bible we discover that it is one exposé or unmasking after another. Adam and Eve in the Garden of Eden had to be flushed out of their hidings. David had to be told by Nathan, after his affair with Bathsheba, "Thou are the man" (II Sam. 12:7). John the Baptist refused baptism to those who had not produced some evidence of genuine repentance (Luke 3:7-15). The Prodigal Son came to himself and then he came clean with his father. And before the Apostle Paul could find peace with God he had to strip away all the facades of righteousness and goodness and ask the very personal question to a voice speaking to him "Who are you, Lord?" (Acts 9:5).

I heard a famous psychiatrist say to a group of psychotherapists, "You never try to remove all of man's hypocrisy; he couldn't stand it." That may be. Religion, however, comes to man who is encased in rationalizations, pretenses, and false roles. It quietly asks man to look at himself and peel off these layers of unnecessary covering and come to know and be the genuine, authentic self which is God's highest creation. The courage to see will necessarily precede "the courage to be." Both will require a piercing pair of fresh eyes.

Maybe I should tell you how I came to select the title of this chapter. A man who used to hear me preach regularly told me the story of his early life. He had gone to the penitentiary in his early twenties for a crime for which he was guilty—embezzlement, but others who escaped imprisonment were equally guilty, and he was extremely bitter.

One day the chaplain talked to him and said, "My boy,

the world is full of injustices and of people who have never been caught. Some of them strut and appear better than they are, but you don't have to let this bother you. It is a great hindrance to a man to have to go through life pretending. They will be pretending. You were guilty and are paying your penalty. When you get out, don't try to pretend that you are not an ex-con. Most people will accept you if you will be yourself. Don't pretend, to either God or man."

I was amazed to learn that this man had served a term in prison. He was a successful and highly respected business man in the community.

Then he said, "I wish you would preach a sermon on 'The Handicap of Our Pretenses.' This is a needed message for our day."

CHAPTER 4

How Christ Helps the Home

I used to tell young couples about to get married that if they would have grace before meals and daily devotions together in their home, their marriages would be appreciably stronger. I emphasized the fact that the way they started off their marriage would likely be the way they would keep it. "Have the blessing at the table the first meal you are together after your honeymoon," I found myself saying to these beginners in marriage.

After over thirty years of listening to hundreds of marital problems, many of whom had tried religious exercises to exorcise the demons that destroy conjugal happiness, I have decided that praying together is not enough. This is not to say that Christian family rituals are of no value. It would seem to me that they are, in fact. However, I cannot say that "the family that prays together will stay together." Too many people have used prayer as a good luck practice; they say a prayer as a kind of guarantee that God won't let them fail even if they practice bad human relations. Such praying will not work. I have known some very mean people do some very loud praying to the great discredit to their religion and to the disdain of their families.

How, then, does Christ help the home? What does Christianity have to contribute to the split-level family in the space age? What difference will it make to your family life whether or not you are a Christian? How can we apply religion, that "best portion of a good man's life," to the way he lives at home?

Thomas Carlyle said over a hundred years ago that "a man's religion is the chief fact with regard to him." And Jonathan Swift over two hundred years ago said, "We have just enough religion to make us hate, but not enough to make us love one another." It would seem to me that, in line with these two quotations, we may set it down as a truism that the best proof of the genuineness of a man's religion is how he practices Christian love within his family circle. If I cannot follow Christ in home living, where can I follow Him?

Unfortunately the approach of much popular religion today is to major on "thou shalt nots," to taboo divorce even though the marriage is destroying the children and one or both mates, and to spend our time fussing about the terrible influence of TV and movies on the modern family.

My opinion is that movies, TV, salacious literature, and high-pressure advertising cannot appreciably affect today's home-life if we inject into family life the spirit and atmosphere which Jesus Christ placed at the center of His religion. Evil can be overcome only by good.

To be specific, Christ is the salvation of the home only if He is allowed to correct His own religion. To this end, I should like to emphasize four aspects of Christianity which apply especially to the home: (1) Christ teaches tenderness;

(2) Christ does not rely on guilt; (3) Christ calls us to freedom; and (4) Christ inspires hope.

Let's begin with tenderness.

Pediatricians speak of children needing TLC (it sounds like a new drug), and they mean simply "tender loving care." They are trying to get the new-born child out of the nursery down the hall, where the relatives ogle through a glass window, and in close to the body of the mother so that the child can experience skin-to-skin relationships. Some pediatricians even refuse to allow the mother to use a bottle to feed the young infant but insist on cup feeding, the primary purpose being that of having the mother, the nurse, or even the father hold the child close while receiving nourishment.

Psychologists have found that white rats will learn faster, remember longer, and have fewer illnesses if they are stroked and patted. One study, by Harry and Margaret Harlow of the University of Wisconsin, experimented with rearing rhesus monkeys in contact with (1) cloth mother substitutes, (2) wire covered mother-looking objects, (3) other monkeys their own age, and (4) their real mothers and normal body contact. They found that those reared by the cloth and the wire mothers were utterly abnormal in three major functions: self-defense, play, and mating.

Rène Spitz compared children reared in a foundling home where there were six nurses to forty-five babies, and a nursing home where they were cared for by their own mothers. By the end of their first year of life those in the foundling home were in "a vitiated physical and mental condition" even though they had received the same food and care otherwise. At the end of three or four years there were similar disparities in development.

What do such experiments have to do with Christ and his approach to the Christian home?

Have you ever noticed how often the Gospel writers speak of Jesus' touching people? You will be amazed if you read the Gospels, noticing this particular detail. "He touched her hand, and the fever left her" (Matt. 8:15). When a leper crept through the crowd and asked for his healing, Jesus "stretched out his hand and touched him" (Matt. 8:3). The crowd brought the blind to him and begged him to touch them (Mark 8:22; Luke 6:19). They touched Him and He touched them. No doubt there were all sorts of magical presuppositions in the people's minds. Today we fear and shun such beliefs. Nevertheless, we still need touching.

One of the most striking scenes in the life of Christ is that of mothers and fathers bringing their little children to Jesus that He might touch them. In an over-protective attitude the disciples were frantically trying to stop the parents, but we read that Jesus became "indignant" and made one of His famous remarks about the kingdom of heaven belonging to little children. Then "he took them in his arms and blessed them, laying his hands upon them" (Mark 10:16).

Paul, and other New Testament authorities, in writing to various groups, often said that they were to greet one another with a holy kiss or with the kiss of love. In that day kissing on the cheek was like shaking hands today. It was more than looking or waving the hand. It involved tenderness, closeness, nearness, and actual body contact.

I knew a young psychiatrist in a state mental hospital who was working in the ward where the very disturbed elderly, most of them women, were residing. Many of them had been pronounced incurably insane twenty years before. I saw him take them upon his lap and rock them, kiss them, pat them, and put his arm around them as they walked. So many of them became well enough to leave the hospital that this psychiatrist's work was written up in *Time* magazine.

One day a pastoral intern said to him, "What you are doing is not orthodox therapy. What does it mean? How are you helping these people? I notice that some of them who have been hearing voices for years are coming back to reality. What are you doing?"

His reply was, "I love them and spank them. These people have regressed to childhood and they have to be related to where they are." Then he said a very shocking thing: "If the church had known how to show love, many of these people would not have come here in the first place."

I'm sure the church is accustomed to having everything wrong blamed on it. The fact is, however, that the church has neglected to show the importance of tenderness in Christian love. It may even be argued that the church has tended to increase the taboo against tenderness which is so prevalent in our culture. In some American churches traditionally the preaching against dancing has been primarily a taboo against tenderness, not able to make the distinction between tenderness and sexuality.

My main point is that the home is the place for tenderness. We have thought of "home, sweet home" as the place of fidelity, economic security, conversation, and mutual courtesy and respect. But these are not enough. Patting, touching, embracing, and any other expressions of genuine affection are a necessary part of Christian family life. Not only do children need it, everyone does. One of the saddest facts about growing old is that older people are so seldom touched. And the husband-wife relationship must be maintained, not only by mutual friends, common interests, and recreational expressions, but by what scientists call tactual contact or stimulation, skin-to-skin relationship.

One woman in marriage counseling said to me, pointing to her forehead, "My husband kisses me right there when he leaves for work; and what good does that do?" A husband says concerning his wife, "If I touch her, she thinks I have ulterior motives. It seems to me that marriage involves affection and that is all I am seeking." A young girl who had failed in her first marriage was trying to understand why she was so cold to her husband. When I asked her to tell me about her relationship with her father she said, "I can never remember sitting in his lap, but I can remember standing around on one foot and then the other at night wishing I could throw my arms around my father's neck. I was afraid to because he was reading and would have blown up." That, in my mind, partly accounted for her frigidity.

Let us turn now to a second way that Christ helps the home. He relied on challenge rather than condemnation to motivate people.

Everyone in the home is concerned for motivating other members of the family. This is not the same as manipulation, or controlling, or maneuvering other people. To motivate may mean merely to create the environment where each can become his whole self without the deterrents of fear, guilt, and appeal to duty. Fear, as John says, "has to do with punishment" (1 John 4:18). Fear says, "If you do not do so-and-so, I will punish you." Guilt says, "Aren't you ashamed of yourself for not performing in such-and-such a way?" Appeal to duty says, "It is your duty to love me or to obey me or to respond to me in a certain way because I am your wife or husband or father or child, etc."

The Christian approach to interpersonal relations is, "I do

not want you to respond to me out of fear of reprisal or feelings of guilt or from duty. If you love me and find me lovable, open to me and reveal yourself to me."

To me it is fascinating that the greatest commandment, according to the Bible, is to love God with all there is within you, and the second is to love your neighbor as one like yourself. These Scriptures are certainly relevant to the home. Between husband and wife, between parent and child, between sibling and sibling, there can never be the issue of duty, or guilt, or judging, or criticism. It must always be: How can you respond? What do you find within yourself for me? Am I worth putting yourself out for? And, do you care enough about me to adapt to me, or to meet me half way?

Generally speaking, family life has been built upon threats or fear of punishment. The child is conditioned to knowing that if he does not do certain things he will be punished in a certain way. Then, hopefully, he is told that if he behaves a certain way he will receive certain rewards.

All too often husbands and wives threaten one another with divorce. "If you step out on me or do not keep house a certain way or if you do not treat my relatives right, I will divorce you." I suppose most couples utter threats of one kind or another during years of marriage. But threats are a poor means of motivation. By threats you may get the other person to give in, but you will rarely accomplish free acts of giving. Most of us can sense the difference between *giving* and *giving in*.

This is not to say that fear or threats have absolutely no place at all in the Christian home. Every parent uses punishments as well as rewards to deter or direct a child. However, challenge rather than condemnation is the goal of interpersonal relations in the Christian family, especially between adults and in dealing with older children.

Jesus gave the epitome of Christian motivation in his remark to his disciples, "If you love me, you will keep my commandments" (John 14:15). Between adults there can be no commands, only requests and invitations. It can be said with equal insight and depth of relationship, "If I love you, I will do what I can to foster your security, satisfaction, self-fulfillment and success." This sounds much better than the if-you-love-me approach. People who devote themselves to loving others without expecting a return, will get back all the love they need.

Challenge, or condemnation? These are the contrasts between Christianity, and paganism. It is the polarity between the Gospel and the law; between freedom and compulsion.

I am amazed at how frequently guilt and shame and threats are used to coerce members of the family. There seems to be a basic unwritten hypothesis in the average American home which reads: "If you want a person to do or be good, make him feel bad about himself." But an appeal to guilt and shame is not Christian. Christians can learn a better way from Christ.

A third distinguishing mark of a Christian home is freedom. I refer to enabling freedom—in contrast with crippling compulsions and sterile lethargy.

Frequently, freedom is equated with impulsiveness and rebellion and anarchy. Obviously, there is a kind of freedom which means to be free from restraints, obligations, and responsibilities. This is the freedom of the delinquent, the criminal, and the dictator. No one in his right mind could advocate such absolute freedom.

The word "freedom" as it is commonly used in the Bible

applies to the significant aspects of human life. When Jesus said, "If the Son makes you free, you will be free indeed," (John 8:36) he was speaking of an inner breadth of feeling that is far beyond rules and rituals. When Paul talks of our being set free from sin and death he was writing of an inner experience that allowed man to move beyond his past shackled life. The Christian concept of freedom, at its deepest level, is more like that of Richard Lovelace's concept which shouts that:

> Stone walls do not a prison make
> Nor Iron bars a cage.

Then proceeds to say:

> If I have freedom in my love,
>   And in my soul am free,
> Angels alone that soar above
>   Enjoy such liberty.

As I view family problems of all sorts, I believe that our greatest problem is in our inability or unwillingness to love from deep within us. Coldness in the home, unfaithfulness between partners, the domination of inlaws, unhealthy rebellion of children, and excessive manipulation of children by parents—these all grow out of enslavements or unfreeness of the individuals involved.

I do not refer here to lack of tenderness, which has already been discussed, nor to the use of guilt to dominate the individuals within the home, both of which are forms of spiritual crippling. Freedom to live and love and be happy is the freedom to live productively within a family group. This freedom is a kind of inner quality that cannot be taught. It grows out of a freeing experience with self and others (including God) which sees clearly that living is loving and loving is living.

This kind of freedom is hinted at by James Oppenheim in "The Slave:"

> They can only set men free . . .
> And there is no need for that:
> Free men set themselves free.[1]

Let me see now if I can tell you how I see Christ helping families become free, how He sets them free. You see freedom in their ability to communicate. Their hearts are open to members of the family, and they are not fearful of being laughed at, scolded, or run off. They share their joys and help each other with their burdens. Even when one member has distorted reality, the others patiently bring his vision back to the facts which must be seen. In an exchange of ideas there is freedom to differ without fear of loss of respect from the other.

Robert Frost caught something of the unselfish freedom of the home at its best:

> Home is the place where, when you have to go there
> They have to take you in.
>   I should have called it
> Something you somehow haven't to deserve.[2]

Even with the plaintive overtones of this passage in "The Death of the Hired Man" one cannot catch the feel of

[1]From *Masterpieces of Religious Verse*, ed. by James D. Morrison. Reprinted by permission of Harper and Row, Publishers, #1397.

[2]From "The Death of the Hired Man" from *Complete Poems* of Robert Frost. Copyright 1930, 1939 by Holt, Rinehart and Winston, Inc. Copyright © 1958 by Robert Frost. Copyright © 1967 by Lesley Frost Ballantine. Reprinted by permission of Holt, Rinehart and Winston, Inc.

uniqueness about the home as he saw it. It is a haven with a unique freedom and acceptance.

Freedom to become all that you can become as a person is involved in family life. "You don't care about me as a person," sobbed one wife to her husband, "all you want is for me to be a showpiece for your business associates and a mother to your children so that people will think you are a great family man." She felt trapped by a lack of freedom.

I could cite hundreds of examples; parents who will not give their children the freedom to choose their own vocations; women who are more concerned for the size of the husband's pay check than whether he is doing what fulfills him in life; parents who thank God that we live in the land of the free so far as worship is concerned, yet do not guide their children to a knowledge of God, but rather lead them to worship nature, or success, or the state.

This by no means is meant to imply that we should not guide our children or advise our mates. Not at all. But guidance and advice does little good unless we can love deeply and frankly.

Christian freedom says, "I want you to become what you truly are, all that you feel you can be, and get the most out of life as you see life." This is very different from the approach which says "You are my wife (or my husband or my child or my father) and I have the right to demand certain things from you." When we are free inside ourselves; free from the law, as Paul would say; free from compulsions and obsessions, as psychologists would say; we can love and live freely with one another in the close, permanent relationship called the home.

A final component which Christ contributes to the home is hope.

There was a time when hope was a word used largely by the clergy. Now psychologists and psychiatrists, as well as pastoral counselors, are saying with the Apostle Paul, "In this hope we were saved" (Rom. 8:24).

I have heard of a series of experiments where rats were placed in pools of water from which there was no possible escape. One experiment was so constructed that it was clearly evident that they were doomed. The other experiment offered an element of hope. Evidence that escape was possible was introduced into it. In the first, the rats gave up and drowned in a comparatively few minutes. In the second, with its element of hope, some were able to swim for as long as fifty hours.

Most medical doctors have seen many patients get well who have a strong hope, while the hopeless will most surely die. Teachers tell of pupils who give up and do much more poorly than their equally talented classmate because hope flags. To be successful, a salesman must keep up hope even when love and faith have weakened.

So it is in the home. There are few family situations which could not be made livable, and some which are presently mediocre which might become magnificent, if hope were present. When I talk to a couple in marriage counseling, I find myself frequently asking during the first or second interview, "Do you feel very hopeful about your future together?" If one or both have lost hope, I know that their task of rebuilding a marriage will be difficult.

Where children are involved in delinquency I try to assess the kind of optimism the parents have about this child's recovery. It is difficult to help children grow up and become responsible people if the parents have already fallen into the despair of those who came to Jesus crying, "Have mercy on my child: for he is a lunatic" (Matt. 17:15). We may think that our children act like lunatics at times, but that label certainly does them no good.

An unfortunate but common attitude often held in marriage may be expressed in these words, "I can tell you one thing about my wife, she will never change. Doctor, I have lived with her for fifteen years and she is like the laws of the Medes and the Persians. She never changes, except possibly for the worst." Where do we get the idea that people cannot change? This is a devastating sort of determinism which may become just a good alibi for not changing.

I insist that there are no hopeless home situations, only people who become hopeless at or about the home. Of course, we get into ruts and try to keep in them in spite of time and tide. It is also true that some people are more open to change than others, and all of us are more creative during some periods in our lives than in others.

Creativity in the home is always the outgrowth of hope. When hope dies, creativity dwindles. When creativity is absent, man never dares the impossible so he does not even accomplish the possible.

"Hope springs eternal in the human breast" the poet (Pope) said. Not necessarily. It sometimes just lies there, guarded by the demons of lethargy and inertia. But in Christ we are inspired to hope—to believe that there is a Christian approach to every problem. I would say "a Christian solution," but this sounds too easy. There is a hopeful way to attack all of our less-than-their-best family situations—even to live peacefully with some of them—but only hope will find the best possible approach.

Today, when sociologists are forcing us to look at the high incidence of broken and unhappy homes; when psychologists are making us suspect our hidden motives in creating such homes; when teachers of social ethics are chiding us for not assuming more responsibility for marriage failures; what shall we as Christians say about ourselves and our neighbors?

We can say, "Where there is hope there is life." No, I did not misquote the proverb. It is hope that sustains life, as well as life that contains hope. Hope, a function primarily of the imagination, projects us toward our Christian goals—created by the imagination in the first place. We are what we hope for in the home. We become what we plan to become.

CHAPTER 5

Everything Nailed Down Is Coming Loose

These are the dramatic words of the Angel Gabriel, look-ing down on the earth's rotten confusion. Marc Connelly in his folksy writing in *Green Pastures* caught more than the Negro theology in his net of simple dialect. He expressed the characteristic feeling about our age.

Whether we call the latter half of the twentieth century the age of anxiety, the age of aspirins, the age of analysis, or the age of the atom, we may be very sure that moorings of the past are loosening. Old landmarks are being removed. Sturdy rafters and solid roof beams are collapsing. Founda-tions are shaking.

A recent cartoon in the *New Yorker* shows a harassed executive lamenting, "Oh, for the good old days when we had nothing to fear except fear itself."

One of the classic statements about man's questing for security is in the Epistle to the Hebrews. It tells about Abra-ham and his family leaving their home in Ur, "not knowing where he was to go." This, the author says, was done by faith. Then he made this remarkably penetrating remark: "He looked forward to the city which has foundations, whose builder and maker is God" (Heb. 11:10).

How could the writer have stated better the hunger for certainty and security than to speak of it as a city with foundations laid by God himself? What Abraham sought all mankind has secretly wished for. But at the same time we also want change and adventure and new frontiers. However, in the conflict between adventure and safety, we tend to become fearful when we see so much change all about us. It would certainly be much more comfortable if a few more things were nailed down and would stay put.

Look at what has come loose in this century so far.

The great empires of England, France, Portugal, and the Netherlands have largely fallen. In 1917 there were 50,000 Communists. Now there are about one billion. The United Nations, still somewhat hanging in the balance, has been born since 1945 when the atomic bomb proved conclusively that war is not the solution to our problems. Africa, like a sleeping giant, has declared to the whole world that things are not what they were.

Today, with the whole earth surrounded by tremulous network of missiles, targets and radar screens, no one can sleep with the same certainty we once had. We are living in the bull's-eye, as the late President Kennedy described it; or to use Dean Rusk's phrase, we are negotiating eyeball to eyeball and each side is afraid to blink. Someone may press a button anytime.

Look at the religious world—The Vatican Council issued some shattering modifications to century-old customs. The Roman Church has opened negotiations on birth control and has broken a thousand-year-old custom of having the mass in

Latin. Protestants no longer fight one another on a large scale and are seriously considering union. Jews, Catholics, and Protestants are beginning to sit down at conference tables and learn from one another. It could be only a matter of time until Muslim, Buddhist, Taoist and Hindu will join the conversation.

Or look at what is happening within our old-line Protestant denominations. The Bible and the message is being re-examined. An occasional heresy hunt occurs in seminaries, but for the most part the church is not afraid to discard old jargon, write new confessions of faith, and recognize the lordship of the living Christ as the way out of defunct ecclesiasticism and churcholatry.

More striking still is the way in which the church has descended from the pulpit and the cloister and marched right out into the voting booth, the slum, and the marketplace to become involved in social and political problems. The church is making its uplifted voice heard and its influence felt by its involvement at the point of need.

Yes, the spirit of change dominates the scene and is expressed daily in the population explosion, the increase in education, the hazards of automation, the sexual revolution, the increase in crime and juvenile delinquency, and in the amazing advances in medical science.

But, let us look now at some of the things in our lives that are nailed down, not coming loose. Yes, things and conditions are changing at a pace never before recorded by man and in more spheres at once, but not everything is coming loose. What is not?

For one thing, the experience of becoming a person remains constant. This does not mean that all babies born into the world grow up to be ever expanding personalities, anymore than all blooms become fruit or all fruits go ahead to ripen. But there are people, perhaps an increasing number of them, who are largely exploring the possibilities of realizing their full potential as human beings. It is not easy to become an authentic person. In fact it is much easier to be an imitator of others, a carbon copy of some hero or heroine, a reflection of what society expects of us.

Lillian Smith in the *Killers of a Dream* says that there are two journeys which every human being must make. One, into himself, accepting what he finds there. The other, into the world, making it his home. It is in this process of adventuring into ourselves and into our world, even into outer space, which remains constant. It is in this process of relating to self, to others, and to things that we experience what might be called personhood.

What I am saying is: the experience of I-ness, of me-ness, is something that remains. In the case of certain types of insanity the self is pretty well fractured and almost collapses, but as I heard a famous psychiatrist say, people do not lose their minds, they simply become overwhelmed and are thrown off balance by the emotions.

Notice some of the great expressions of personhood found in the Bible.

"I am the way, the truth and the life" (John 14:6). Did any person in history have such a sense of selfhood as Jesus? He is the way, or road. Without Him there is no reliable going. He is the truth. This word, used ambiguously so often, must define a perspective that makes meaning out of our puzzling existence. Without the truth there is no knowing. He is the life: life of such exuberance and such conscious depth that only the living of it can prove its validity. Jesus *was* these and *means* these to us. Everyone of us *are* and *mean* some-

thing. It is this becoming and meaning that is sure and stead-
fast, nailed down. We are self-conscious selves in the process
of being persons.

Paul at one point said "I have learned, in whatever state I
am, to be content. I know how to be abased, and I know how
to abound; in any and all circumstances I have learned the
secret of facing plenty and hunger, abundance and want."
(Phil. 4:11-12). Here is the self poised, perhaps poised for
the next shock, the next betrayal, the possible failure, the
subsequent success, the proximate opportunity. Here was a
Christian, if we can accept his testimony at face value, who
had committed himself to reality without reservation. He
must have believed that it was a reality aimed and guided
toward constructive and not intolerable goals.

His secret is found in this statement: "I can do all things
in him who strengthens me" (Phil. 4:13). Today, caught up
in the cult of self-reliance, we tend to say, "I can do all things
if I believe in myself enough." Self-trust is important. Many
people have not gotten even that far. But one can do only as
much by himself as his own strength, his nature and talents
will allow. By calling on a Higher Power he may do what
otherwise would have been impossible. This has always been
the goal of Christianity—to accomplish the otherwise impossible.

Another constant in this world of vocal variables, is the
possibility of transcendence. To transcend means to rise
above, to overcome something. It is almost a modern term.
Until recently technocracy has not enabled us to rise very
high, physically. When man rode a horse he was taller and
surer of foot. With the invention of gun powder he length-
ened his arm to strike. Only in the space age has he soared
into outer space. Perhaps now his spirit or character can be-

gin ascent. But ascent is not the primary goal of the human spirit. It is possible to ascend without having much regard for that which is around us, without ever admitting involvement. The Christian is very much besieged by the problems and stresses around him, but he has the resources to rise above, manage, cope with his tempestuous environment. "Be of good cheer, I have overcome the world", Jesus said. (John 16:33, RSV).

There are three deadly, damaging, debilitating experiences that human beings need to transcend, at least three that I am thinking of at this moment. Delay, disappointment, and discouragement. It is in the process of facing these dragons of the spirit that we become whole selves. The possibility of transcendance is a constant factor in man's experience every moment of his life experience.

Browning caught the spirit of what is permanent in "Rabbi Ben Ezra." He said: "Earth changes, but the soul and God stand sure." This may sound like begging the question to many people—drawing a conclusion from a premise that needs to be proved as much as the conclusion. But, I am not trying to draw a conclusion or prove that there is a God. Nothing is quite so futile. Even if I could intellectually prove the fact of God, nothing would have changed except that we would hold in our minds one more concept or opinion.

Rather, the Christian (and Jewish) experience of God is that of standing before him; confrontation. You may say that your neighbors do not exist; that these objects you see walking about are not really persons. After all, what do you see except skin and eyes and hair and clothes; objects moving about and making certain sounds? But even while you are saying that you cannot prove your neighbors' existence, you believe deep down in your hearts that your neighbors are real persons like yourselves. As Pascal said, "The heart has reasons that the mind does not know."

A. N. Whitehead noted that religion passes from God the void to God the enemy and from Him to God the companion. This is the way most adults experience God, if they experience Him at all; but however they experience God, it is always God above and beyond time and transitoriness.

> Swift to its close ebbs out life's little day;
> Earth's joys grow dim, its glories pass away;
> Change and decay in all around I see:
> O Thou who changest not, abide with me.

> Henry Francis Lyte, "Abide With Me"
> 2nd Stanza

"In the beginning God." It is both impossible to conceive of a world without a beginning, or of what would be beyond a beginning if one did exist. This, then, is the Bible's way of saying that somewhere the mind comes to a jumping off place, and there stands God. There is no way for us to think of God except in terms of the way we think, in terms of persons and things. So, I conclude without apology: at the outside entrance door of history stood God.

You recall the experience of Moses in the desert when he felt commissioned to lead a host of slaves out of Egypt. The Voice said to Moses, that when Pharoah asks who sent you, "I am that I am." Some have translated it, "I will be what I will be." The late Martin Buber says it should read "I shall be there" *(Eclipse of God,* p. 53).

I like that. It is God's personal existence as experienced by Moses and multitudes since as present, everlasting, always existent, the Eternal One. As Buber, a Jewish philosopher himself, says, the God of Abraham, God of Isaac, and God of

Jacob "cannot be reduced to a God of the philosophers." He is more than Primum Movum, or First Cause, more than the World Soul or Supreme Being.

In the last chapter of Hebrews, there is an appeal to the early Jewish Christians to stand by their faith. The author refers to the victory of their leaders over history. "Consider," he says, "the outcome of their life" (13:7). Then he hits the bull's eye of truth in one comprehensive statement: "Jesus Christ is the same yesterday and today and forever" (v. 8). A little farther in the same passage the writer says: "Here we have no lasting city, but we seek the city which is to come" (v. 14).

Any way we look at it, we are dependent on something outside ourselves. We all know that. We tend, and have from at least the times of the ancient Stoics, to put a capital letter on the word Nature and talk about the laws and the course of nature. But unless some benevolent God is running the show, there may be forces in our world which will cause a disintegration at any moment. Or with the splitting of the atom it would not be too difficult for man to destroy all the life upon this planet.

Our imagination falters when we think on what man will do to man and to life upon this planet. My hope is in the fact that God is working and that He will keep on working in our lives. Some of us memorized Romans 8:28 as saying "All things work together for good to them that love God." The Revised Standard Version, besides being a better translation, gets to the real meaning of faith in God as the One who causes history to turn out right. It reads "We know that in everything God works for good with those who love him." There is no assurance that things will work for good unless a good God is doing the working. In a world of change, when everything seems to be coming loose, there "stands God within the shadow keeping watch above his own." Or as Tennyson stated: "Cast all your cares on God; that anchor holds." (*Enoch Arden*). We can understand how the little girl during the bombings in London in World War II, prayed: "O God, take good care of yourself for if something happens to You, we are sunk." There's one certainty in this world of eruption and change: certain relationships will last forever.

The basic fear of human beings is isolation. We can stand anything but aloneness. Actually, one study shows that we can stand that only a few days at the most without becoming seriously disturbed. There are no Robinson Crusoes except in fiction.

Another terrifying fear for the human being is that of falling into the hands of enemies, to be among those who will reject him. Hell must be a place of continuous indifference. We can stand to be alone if we have hope of finding someone to relate to, or we can stand to fight with people if we think that ultimately we can either turn them into friends, or slay them, or escape them and find home base where someone is awaiting us.

I believe that there are three experiences described in the Bible which are not transitory, that last. One is the Word; it is eternal. The second is the church; death cannot destroy it. The third is heaven; the eternal dwelling place of God and of His people. Jesus said more than once, "Heaven and earth will pass away, but my words will not pass away" (Matt. 5:18; 24:35; Luke 16:17). He said of the church that "the gates of hell shall not prevail against it;" or as the Revised Standard Version translates it: "On this rock I will build my church, and the powers of death shall not prevail against it" (Matt. 16:18). Many passages speak of "my Father's house;"

and "these go away into life eternal;" and "nothing can separate us from the love of God, not death nor anything else in all creation." The Book of Revelation pictures a city where people shall dwell with God without pain or grief or tears.

From this we see that God by His word creates the church, forms relationships which shall never be broken in this world or in the world to come. Heaven means permanency of relationship. The church is a relationship of people under the Lordship of Christ, bound together by love and self-giving.

Permanent relationships are only possible between people who are basically good, good in the sense that they are willing to respect one another, leave each other free, give of themselves graciously to one another and acknowledge their indebtedness to one another. Even in this world of crime, selfishness, hate, insecurity, and destruction there are so many good people, people of compassion and concern.

This is not to say that people are all that way. One of my friends who is President of a Christian College in the deep South was asked if he believed in hell. He had grown up in a period of extreme liberalism even though he belonged to a very conservative (theologically) denomination. His reply was: "Well, I'll tell you. There was a time when I didn't believe in hell, but I've seen so many so-and-so's (actual words omitted) that I have decided there must be a hell. If these people were turned loose in heaven, they would soon mess it up."

But in spite of such people in the world and the sorrow and suffering and insecurity that they cause, I still believe that when everything else seems to be coming loose there will always be permanency of relationships within the church. It may be that our present organizations will not survive. God may set aside or by-pass the organized church as we know it, but I have every confidence that the event which began with Christ coming into this world will continue. Faith, hope, and love relationships will remain. This is the city which has lasting foundations.

In Huntsville, Missouri, a little town near Moberly, there is a ninety-seven year old man who attends the Baptist Church every Sunday even though he cannot hear a word of the sermon. Someone asked him, "Why do you go to church every Sunday when you can't hear?" His reply was: "I want people to know which side I am on in this world." It is this kind of person who will stand firm when everything seems to be coming loose.

CHAPTER 6

I Need All the Friends I Can Get

This amusing bit of dialogue appears in the delightful cartoon book by Charles Schultz entitled *I Need All The Friends I Can Get*.

Charlie Brown says to Lucy, "I don't have any friends . . . I don't have one single person I can call a friend."

Lucy says, "Define 'Friend'!"

Then a number of very striking definitions of friend are given:

"A friend is someone who will take the side with the sun in his eyes." (He has a tennis racket in his hand and is looking across the net).

"A friend is someone who's willing to watch the program you want to watch" (on TV).

"A friend is someone who can't stand the same sort of music you can't stand!"

"A friend is someone who sticks up for you when you're not there."

"A friend is someone who accepts you for what you are."

At one point Lucy says, "I think you try too hard, Charlie Brown . . . Be like me, I don't need any friends . . . I'm self-sufficient!"

"Not me . . ." he says, "I need all the friends I can get! I'd even settle for a 'fair-weather' friend."

Lucy says, as she walks away, "Poor ol' Charlie Brown . . . He really should try to be like me. I don't care if I have any friends or not . . . Just so I'm popular!"

Charlie Brown's response is, "I don't know . . . Talking to her never does much for me . . ." Later he says, "All these definitions have got me confused."[1]

Definitions of friendships are much easier to come by than illustrations of friendship. This is not to say that friendly acts are uncommon. However, there is a great deal of difference between being friendly and being a friend. "Little, nameless, unremembered acts of kindness and of love" (Wordsworth) are not all there is to friendship.

Absolutely no one in all of history proclaimed, demonstrated, illustrated, lived, and died for friendship as did Jesus of Nazareth. He was the friend of tax collectors and sinners. They scandalized Him by saying that He "receives sinners and eats with them." Even in the moment of Judas' most wicked betrayal, Jesus called him "friend." Nothing could cause Him to turn a friend into an enemy.

After Jesus had endowed the very word "friend" with new meaning, He said to His disciples:

> This is my commandment, that you love one another as I have loved you. Greater love has no man than this, that a man lay down his life for his friends. You are my friends if

---

[1]Charles M. Schulz, *I Need All The Friends I Can Get* (San Francisco: Determined Production, Inc.). © 1964 by United Feature Syndicate.

you do what I command you. No longer do I call you servants, for the servant does not know what his master is doing; but I have called you friends, for all that I have heard from my Father I have made known to you. You did not choose me, but I chose you and appointed you that you should go and bear fruit and that your fruit should abide; so that whatever you ask the Father in my name, he may give it to you. This I command you, to love one another (John 15:12-17).

I shall try to show that Jesus revealed the very essence of friendship and practiced it in three dimensions. To Him, friendship involved self-disclosing, self-giving, and self-sustaining. These principles are necessary to being true friends.

Before we look deeper at Jesus' concepts let us remember the long history of the idea of friendship. The Bible says of Moses that the Lord spoke unto him "face to face, as a man speaketh with a friend" (Ex. 33:12). Abraham was called, according to James, "the friend of God" because he believed God and obeyed Him (Jas. 2:22). And the writer of the Proverbs says one of the most profound things that has ever been written on the subject:

A man that hath friends must show himself friendly: and there is a friend that sticketh closer than a brother (Proverbs 18:24 KJV).

This is an old theme. Hesiod who lived in the eighth century before Christ wrote:

When on your home falls unforeseen distress,
Half-clothed come neighbors, kinsmen stay to dress.
Works and Days

Aristotle in *Nichomachaen Ethics* wrote on this theme.

Cicero wrote one of his greatest essays *(De Amicitia)* on friendship. Among other things he said, "A friend is, as it were, a second self."

In modern times who has not read Emerson's famous essay, entitled "Friendship?" He called a friend "a masterpiece of Nature." High friendship, he said, demands the "ability to do without it." "A friend is a person with whom I may be sincere. Before him, I may think aloud." "I do then with my friends as I do with my books. I would have them where I can find them, but I seldom use them."

Two recent books that deal with two of our societies' most pressing problems—family life and mental health—give a primary place to friendship. I refer to *Successful American Families*, by Zimmerman and Cervantes; and William Schofield's *Psychotherapy—The Purchase of Friendship*.

The first of these, by two Harvard sociologists, studied 60,-000 American families in such diverse places as Boston, New Orleans, Denver, Stillwater, Oklahoma, and Morgantown, West Virginia. They found that families which had five or more friend-families (units) were more likely to be successful. The isolated family is the one most likely to be in trouble. Rich friendships which last ten years or more are characteristic of strong family life, as well as a safeguard against family failure.

Also in Dr. Schofield's book (he, a clinical psychologist and professor in the Department of Psychiatry of the University of Minnesota Medical School), we see how imperative friendship is. After admitting that if all of the people who need treatment for emotional problems were to turn to the presently trained psychiatrists, psychologists, and counselors, we would not begin to have enough therapists to treat them; he talks about the "invisible therapists." They are the many people who are regularly turned to for friendship, for guidance and counsel, and who give it.

Instead of saying that it is dangerous to tell your problems to a friend or relative, Schofield says: "It is a proper part of mental hygiene for the individual to understand the necessity for and functions of friendship, and to be encouraged to look to friends for something more than playful companions." He is not belittling trained therapists. Rather, he is saying what we need is more trained *friendshippers.*

In the light of the needs and the tremendous challenges of the lonely, alienated culture in which we live, let us examine some of the penetrating insights of Jesus on this subject. The New English Translation of this first concept involved in friendship reads: "I have disclosed to you everything that I heard from my father" (John 15:15). Disclosed. That is the heart of the matter.

Any human being hides from, keeps secrets from, three classes of people. Those who are enemies and might use his secrets against him. Those who are beneath him, and he deems not worth his self-revelation. Or those who are strangers, and he does not know whether they would be appreciative or hostile.

Why do people hide from one another or turn their backs to one another or look past one another? They fear. Risk is involved. They may get hurt.

In the movie, *Young Lovers,* there is the dialogue: "You have injured me . . . a friend is one who can be injured by another". Right! When I see people who are so calloused that no one can hurt them, I feel sorry for them. They do not know how to bleed. No one can hurt them because they refuse to care for another deeply, and even though they may lose no blood they will reach no depth in a relationship.

One of my counselees raged at his wife when she had angered him, "I hate you; I hate you; you have made me feel. No one has ever made me feel before. I cannot afford to feel either love nor hate." Later in the privacy of a counseling session, he told me how his father had kicked him in the nose once when he was cleaning up something off the kitchen floor. He ran two blocks away from home. At ten years that was about as far as he could go and be safe. But he vowed, half-consciously, that he would never show his feelings again.

My point is that people are deathly afraid of revealing themselves to one another. They fear being laughed at, ignored, thought stupid, or even classified as sick.

Altogether too few people have the grace to accept another human being in all of his complexity, in his perversity even, and especially in his oddity. We come at one another with little photographs (or movies) of how we think the other person ought to be or act. When they fail us, we condemn them or lecture them or turn away in indifference—this last is the essence of inhumanity and the hallmark of irreligion.

There is a story that comes out of the near east which tells of an Arab travelling in the desert. He sees something in the distance. His first remark is, "It is a mirage." Then he soon exclaims, "It is a monster." Later, "No, it is a man." As the image moves closer he exclaims, "It is my brother."

This is what Matthew Arnold meant by "the same heart beats in every human breast." We hunger to know one another. We long for someone who has the courage to tell us what he really thinks and feels and sees and wishes and hopes for.

Jesus was expressing one of the profound aspects of friendship when He said that He did not treat the disciples like servants who needed to know only the orders of life—

He was revealing the secrets. A friend is one who opens his heart to you.

A friend is self-giving. Jesus' words, "Greater love has no man than this, that a man lay down his life for his friends" (John 15:13) have become classic. How could the statement be made stronger. We say, "A friend in need is a friend indeed;" and, "You never know who your friends are until adversity strikes." What Jesus is saying, however, is much more profound. His meaning is that the very nature of being or having a friend is that you give of yourself, lay down your life—not only if it is necessary, but continuously, in the act of befriending.

James Russell Lowell said it succinctly in "The Vision of Sir Launfal:"

> The gift without the giver is bare;
> Who gives himself with his alms, feeds three,
> Himself, his hungering neighbor, and me.

And Stevenson wrote "No man is useless while he has a friend." This last quotation implies both the quality of being befriended as giving meaning to a life and, equally important, the compelling fact that as long as you have a friend, you have the opportunity and necessity of giving of yourself, which may well be the supreme meaning of life.

Perhaps we can best understand self-giving by way of contrast. Some give merely to get back from the recipient, this is swapping or moral shrewdness. Some give things or services but never allow themselves to become involved in deep social concerns. Such giving may be useful, but it certainly has a different dimension from self-giving. Others practice what may be called mimic morality or imitation service—going through one good deed after another like a robot. Their motives may be self-aggrandisement, a mere discharge of nervous energy, an attempt to cover up or atone for guilt, or even an effort to gain a reputation as a "good guy."

Not all giving is self-giving. Actually, costly gifts for which one sacrifices may be merely a substitute for the giving of self. Unfortunately, many parents give their children toys, ponies, books, trips, automobiles but they never get around to giving time, affection, conversation, or an eager ear.

Jesus struck at phony giving when he instructed His disciples about their social practices. When you prepare a dinner or banquet, do not invite your relatives or rich neighbors or friends, but the poor and the crippled and the blind. "They cannot repay you." (See Luke 14:12-14). The good deed done for bad reasons, or the right act performed from the wrong motive, or high moral standards maintained out of pride or fear—these all fall short of Christian morality.

Self-giving means *putting yourself out* for another person who needs you. It involves the overcoming of self so we can concentrate on persons who confront us. It means really *seeing* the needs of the world and stepping out boldly to meet them. Self-giving means responding to persons and situations without reference to what-do-I-get-out-of-it; or what-will-it-cost-me? Paul said that Jesus is to be our great example here "who, though he was in the form of God, did not count equality with God a thing to be grasped, but emptied himself," (Phil. 2:6-7).

The *graspers* and *emptiers,* those who hold on to their lives and those who lay down their lives, those who save their lives and those who lose them—these are the great contrasts in human living. I do not think for a moment that the implication is that friendship is expressed primarily in terms of martyrdom. Let's face it: Few people are confronted with either the invitation to or the opportunity for dying for a cause. In many instances, this might well be easier than living for one. There is certainly no doubt that it would take courage to risk one's life for a friend or a cause, but it also takes courage, patience, and a special kind of mature love to be a self-giving friend. I wonder if there aren't circumstances where the self-giving life is greater than the self-giving death?

Albrecht Durer was born in 1471 in Germany. His close friend was a young man whom we know only by the name of Hans. They were struggling artists, trying desperately to support themselves while they studied, but work kept them from classes.

One day Hans, the older of the two, proposed that Albrecht devote all his time to study while he, Hans, work to support them both. Years passed. Albrecht studied in the great cities of Europe and became one of the great painters of his day. Hans through rough, manual labor to support his friend, ended up with gnarled, stiff fingers that could not wield the artist's brush in the slender strokes necessary to effective painting.

Out of a heart overflowing with love and gratitude Albrecht Durer immortalized those hands on the canvas. His "Praying Hands" tells the eloquent story of self-giving, and succeeding generations have been enriched by this masterpiece of art.

Jesus pointed out another characteristic of friendship— *self-sustaining friendship*. "You did not choose me, but I chose you" (John 15:16). This central idea is seen repeatedly in the Gospel story. A moving expression of this is seen in John 13:1: ". . . when Jesus knew that his hour had come to depart out of this world . . . having loved his own who were in the world, he loved them to the end." By contrast with the way most of us operate, this is indeed a quality of friendship which is "out of this world."

There are three varieties of so-called friendship frequently seen today: fair weather friendship, no-boundary friendship, and tete-à-tete friendship. Unfortunately, most of us are very familiar with fair weather friendships. Be successful and popular and fair weather friends will gather around like bees in a honeysuckle vine. But just let a man lose his job, or become a figure in scandal, or lose an election, or flunk out at school, or get arrested for a crime, and fair weather friends will scatter like people fleeing the area of an active volcano.

Descriptive of this is the story of the man who ran for the office of sheriff and was overwhelmingly defeated at the polls. The next day he was seen on the streets with a pistol strapped on his side. When an acquaintance asked why he was wearing the gun, he replied, "Wal, I got it figured that any man who doesn't have any more friends than I have had better carry a gun to protect himself."

Jesus warned His disciples that they would be hated—that they would not be surrounded by friends in this world. He pointed out that they would fare no better than He had, and that since He was hated, they could expect to be. And He even went so far as to say, "He who hates me hates my Father also" (John 15:23).

So often people become embittered because of betrayal by some friend. It seems that Jesus is saying to his disciples, "This is the way the world is. They will hate you without a cause. Don't be naïve and you will not be numbed by the experiences of life where someone turns against you."

In Dostoevski's *The Brothers Karamazov* Ivan says to

his priest-brother: "It is not that I don't accept God, you must understand; it is the world created by him I don't and cannot accept." Anyone who has dealt with bitter, disenchanted people, or looked at the cynicism in his own soul, knows that the deep injustices which rankle and sour us are not tornadoes, cyclones, brain tumors, earthquakes, idiot children, or floods; it is man's inhumanity to man. And probably the bitterest experience of all is when a friend turns against us.

In some ways *no-boundary friends* are less devastating, but they certainly can be more of a nuisance. Seemingly oblivious to the fact that friendship does not preclude all privacy, they may look in your refrigerator, open your medicine cabinet, ask you about your will, advise you about what kind of car to buy, and instruct you in religion. On occasion they may pick your emotional pockets and even volunteer opinions about your sex life. It seems that no one ever succeeded in impressing them with the notion that advice should be withheld unless requested.

Then, there are the face-to-face (tete-à-tete) friends. Out of sight out of mind is evidently their slogan. They will wine you and dine you when you are in their town, but forget to call you when they pass through your city. Such people are totally insensitive to the meaning of depth relationships. They swim with the tide, blow hot and cold depending on their superficial moods, but fail to relate warmly and permanently to anyone.

A European had been in this country only a short time when he went into a bar in a great Eastern city. He fell into conversation with an American and they clicked. Each found the other extremely interesting. After the bar closed, they walked for an hour or so in the cool, crisp night air, still enthralled in conversation. Suddenly the American hailed a cab and went away into the night without leaving a card, his telephone number or anything. The European was stunned and grieved. They had hit it off so well together and had, apparently, come to admire each other so abruptly. Did friendship mean so little to Americans? he kept asking himself. Did his new found friend not really care for him? It saddened him.

Really, the important point here is that Jesus' friendship pattern called for a quality that resides in the friend—it is self-sustaining. You see, if I passively wait for someone to show me friendship, I have failed to really comprehend the deep meaning of the word "friend." On the other hand, if I abandon, forsake, or neglect a friend, I have proved that the *residence* of friendship is outside myself.

Friendship is not only self-disclosing and self-giving, it is self-sustaining. This is what Jesus meant in the Sermon on the Mount when He said, "If you exchange greetings only with your own circle, are you doing anything exceptional?" (Matt. 5:47, Phillips). This reminds us of the proverb which says "Friendship is either found among equals or it makes equals of those it finds." There must be something in our Christian concept of "friend" that goes beyond reciprocity. The Christian is to be a self-starter and a self-sustainer.

The writer of Proverbs says, "A friend loveth at all times." Can you beat that? Here is the ideal of friendship that man has reached for through the centuries. It is what we urgently need but seldom find. However, this is precisely what the Christian finds in Christ—a God who loves at all times. Furthermore, He longs for His children to express and practice unconditional and unlimited friendship in every life relationship.

Cicero commented with perceptive insight, "What sweetness is left in life, if you take away friendship? Robbing life of friendship is like robbing the world of the sun." In response to Mrs. Robert Browning's request, "Tell me the secret of your life, so that I may make my life beautiful too," Charles Kingsley replied, "I had a friend."

An unknown poet understood the authentic quality of friendship when he wrote:

> Oh this world's a curious compound,
> With is honey and its gall,
> With its bitter cares and crosses,
> But a good world after all.
> And a good God must ha' made it,
> Leastways, thats what I say
> When a hand's upon my shoulder
> In a friendly sort o' way.[2]

[2]"Fellowship," Unknown, THE BEST LOVED POEMS OF THE AMERICAN PEOPLE, selected by Hazel Felleman, Garden City Books, Garden City, New York, Copyright, 1936, by Doubleday & Company, Inc.

CHAPTER 7

Forgive From Your Hearts

"This is how my Heavenly Father will treat you unless you each forgive your brother from your heart" (Matt. 10:35, Phillips).

Here is the penetrating and startling climax and conclusion to a story Jesus told one day in response to Peter's question: "Master, how many times can my brother wrong me and I must forgive him?" (Matt. 18:21, Phillips).

In the first movements of this narrative Jesus told the king who decided to settle all of his accounts with his various servants. Among them was a poor fellow who owed the king an enormous amount of money. Unfortunately, he had no means or resources for repaying the debt. In pronouncing judgment the king ordered that the debtor, his wife, and children be sold as slaves. He further ordered that whatever possessions the man had be sold and that the money received from all of the transactions be turned over to him in satisfaction of the debt. In agony and desperation the debtor pleaded for mercy. So effective was his plea that the king, in a magnanimous display of pity and compassion, set him free and canceled the entire debt.

Now the scene shifts and we see this same servant in a violent confrontation with one of his associates who owed him a very small amount. When the servant's "friend" could not pay off the small debt, his pleas for mercy were contemptuously ignored, and the miserable fellow was tossed into prison until the debt could be paid.

When their neighbors and fellow servants heard about this despicable miscarriage of justice, they reported the incident to their king. In obvious fury the king called the first servant to account, and after berating him for failing to show the same quality of mercy he had received, he was sentenced to jail until the full amount of his original debt could be paid.

It was at this point that Jesus declared that this was precisely how God would treat a debtor "unless you each forgive your brother *from your heart*."

There is so much misunderstanding of what forgiveness really means that we dare not assume that since the word "forgive" is in common usage, we all mean the same thing by it.

We've all heard the common expression, "forgive and forget." Really now, are these two words synonymous or even closely related? The great preacher of the last century, Henry Ward Beecher, said: " 'I can forgive but I cannot forget' is but another way of saying, 'I cannot forgive.' " Such a remark is both absurd and wide of the mark of forgiveness. It is absurd because even a child knows that he can no more *make* himself forget than he can jump out of his skin. It misses the real focus of forgiveness because forgiveness does not have to do with an event that has occurred. It has to do with caused inner suffering and the reknitting of a re-

lationship which has been torn asunder or seriously ruptured.

True, people who truly forgive tend to forget, depending
on whether they are the cautious type of person or not. When
a person says, "I don't think I can ever forget what has been
done to me," my answer is, "Remember it if you wish, but
can you truly identify with the person who wronged you?
Can you stand in his shoes and realize that you are cut
from the same cloth but by a little different pattern?" Only
God can forget. "I will remember their sins and their mis-
deeds no more" (Heb. 10:17).

When you deal intimately with human beings, as in counseling, you wonder at times if forgiveness is not as rare as
hen's teeth. People bury hatchets but carefully tuck away the
map which tells where their hidden weapon lies. We put our
resentments in cold storage and then pull the switch to let
them thaw out again. Our grudges are taken out to the lake
to drown them—even the lake of prayer—and we end up giving them a swimming lesson. How often we have torn up the
canceled note but hang on to the waste basket that holds the
pieces. This is not to say that human forgiveness does not
occur; only that it is rare and that much that passes for forgiveness is often not so at all.

It may be helpful to look at some examples of pseudo-
forgiveness. I refer to those human experiences which may
be considered forgiveness but actually distort the wonderful meanings of true forgiveness.

Surely, one such misconception is the notion that when you
are forgiven the hurt of offense is canceled or undone. Impossible! The past cannot be undone anymore than you can
revoke the law of gravity. What has occurred will remain as
having occurred forever. But, your reaction to it, or percep-

tion of it, or interpretation of it may change, and does, in forgiveness. Recall if you will the words of the song, "He breaks the power of canceled sin." This is an unscriptural idea; sin cannot possibly be *canceled*. Slaves may be bought out of bondage (redeemed). Judges may declare, for purposes of reforming the individual, that a criminal be treated as if not guilty (justification). A person may start all over again and by the help of God be changed at the core of his being (the new birth). But canceling what has occurred, making it as if it had not happened, this is faulty reasoning and unnecessary theology.

Another expression of pseudo-forgiveness is the act of simply passing over the broken relationship, the offense. A very passive person might say: "Oh, well, whatever was intended, let's just overlook it or pass it by. Often this is just sheer lack of backbone and an apathetic unwillingness to do anything about the situation. This attitude may stem from an indifference to moral issues or from an ignorance of depth interpersonal relations. When one can say, "Oh, it doesn't matter; forget it," it is likely there was not an occasion for forgiveness in the first place.

Condescension is another form of pseudo-forgiveness. It says, "You have hurt me deeply, but I will bear it sweetly." Actually, this is nothing more than a kind of revenge. *Forgive your enemies*. What a marvelous way to parade your superiority and make him feel small. To forgive without understanding the enemy, getting involved with him, and coming to grips with the problem is simply a way of playing God; it is not the way God acts.

Now let us turn our attention to quasi-forgiveness. In its many forms this can assume some of the aspects of mature forgiveness, but it misses the heart of the matter. For example, explaining away what happened is one of these quasi-situations.

"I know now why my husband was unfaithful to me," a woman remarked to her marriage counselor, "so I can forgive him; he was neurotic." She had found a nice label. It gave her an out because she did not really want to punish him or leave him in the first place. As we shall see later, finding a rationale is a part of true forgiveness also—hence the term *quasi*. To explain away personal injury, however, either means that the injury was purely an accident, therefore no forgiveness is needed, or it infers that the offender may not be a responsible person so judgment should be withheld to avoid being unfair to him. So we just say, "He probably couldn't help it; forget it." Such an attitude tends to obscure moral issues and create superficiality in relationships. You either have been offended or hurt, or you have not. If you have, and to the extent that you have, face up to it and attempt a reconciliation.

Another quasi-type of forgiveness which often passes for the real McCoy occurs when a person forgives with reservations. "I will forgive you now, but if it ever happens again, I will retaliate in full force." This lacks something. *Throwing up the past* is one example of forgiveness with reservations; holding a person under suspicion is another. A third one is, that of never really warming up to the offended person again.

A woman remarked to the counselor, "Can we ever have the kind of marriage we once had?" He replied, "I don't know. You might. But if you can be patient while you are finding yourselves and if you truly forgive, you may have a much richer marriage—not the same as before, but better."

It is easy enough to say that since you have been hurt in a particular way, you will never trust this person again as you did before, but that is beside the point. You may have trusted him (or her) unrealistically. The question is, can you relate to this person without reservations that pertain to the offense and to your suffering?

It must be evident from what we have said so far that any occasion which calls for forgiveness is one that involves two basic elements: hurt and estrangement. In the course of events someone is injured and two people are apart. Now, if relationships did not matter, if man and man (as well as man and God) did not belong together—related—there would be no point to forgiveness. When something estranging happens between one person and another, one would simply go off to himself or find someone else to relate to, if relationships did not matter. But they do, to most people.

There is a type of person who says "I have never forgiven anyone or had an occasion to; nor have I ever asked for forgiveness. I never get hurt or intentionally hurt anyone else. All of this talk about forgiveness is irrelevant to me." That is true. He has never loved deeply enough to be hurt. You have to care and attach and feel the indebtedness of a relationship before you can be hurt.

On the other hand many people get hurt over nothing. They feel sorry for themselves, expect other people to wait upon them, and see God as the Supreme Nipple. Injustices are accumulated, and they act like a wet-diapered child when the normal painful events of life occur to them—even God owes them an apology for creating such men in such a world. This type of person is not in a forgiveness situation. Like the person who cannot be hurt, they are either sick, or immature, or spiritually deformed.

Real hurts, experienced by normal people may range from getting your dog run over by the neighborhood drunk, to having your best friend alienate the affection of your wife. But when an authentic injury occurs, you face one of four alternatives: forthright revenge or retaliation; deny the fact of the hurt and repress it (push it out of awareness) if possible; adopt one of the pseudo or quasi approaches; or postpone retribution. The first and last of these alternatives are the ways of law, justice, and punishment. They are very old and very common, but they do not work.

Yet many people are downright afraid to come out wholeheartedly for forgiveness. Some modern religious psychologists, for example, try to make reconciliation by grace mean the same as forgiveness by deserving it on a basis of doing penance for the wrong, making up "for the negative, destructive things he has done in the past."[1] The fear seems to be that if the sinner (or acting-out person) finds out that he will be accepted on the basis of repentance he will go ahead and sin with the tacit (perhaps unconscious) understanding that he will be accepted anyway. This is a gross misunderstanding of repentance and a pathetic distrust of the power of love. It would seem that even a brief review of criminology and child discipline patterns would convince us of the error of the punishment techniques.

A mother, father, and three children sat quietly in a pew listening to what most people thought was a rather good sermon on the Prodigal Son and the Elder Brother (Luke 15). The emphasis was on the fact that people today have their own individual ways of failing, like alcoholism, sexual immorality, homosexuality, dishonesty, laziness and the like. The church too often, the minister said, has confronted these people with a stern, "look, we have stayed at home and be-

[1] O. Hobart Mowrer, *The New Group Therapy* (D. Van Nostrand Company, Inc., 1964), pp. 33-34, 241.

haved ourselves and lived by self-discipline; who are you to expect us to receive you with open arms?" So, said the earnest clergyman, the world stays in the far country and leaves us to our aloof righteousness.

When the father got home, he gathered the children in the living room and said, "I want to clear up some things that were said in the sermon this morning. The pastor forgot to tell you that the Elder Brother did a noble thing by staying home and working hard. Our world is where it is now because we have been too soft with wrongdoers. There is no excuse for prodigal sons. What matters in this world is the very thing the pastor seemed to belittle, self-discipline." The father's face was hard and drawn. The children felt confused. It didn't pay to argue with father. He seemed so sure of himself. The mother overheard the conversation in the kitchen and prayed that somehow her husband might understand the meaning of grace.

The Christian alternative for those who "return" is always forgiveness. But we should not claim forgiveness as the exclusive property of Christianity or even of religion. Most cultures have it as at least a minor part of their value system. But the Christian puts forgiveness at the very center of his religion because he understands that religion means relatedness and to avoid or neglect or break relationships is the essence of sin. Nothing worse lies in the cup of human badness.

Alexander Pope was succinct in the words: "To err is human—to forgive, divine." And our most frequently repeated prayer says, "Forgive us our trespasses as we forgive those who trespass against us."

In a most important book written on the subject of forgiveness, the author says, "The irrelevance of the church in the modern day is the failure of the church to understand the reality of forgiveness. As a living experience, forgiveness is needed and is relevant to the condition of man. Without it, man cannot live; without it, he cannot grow." Thus James G. Emerson, Jr., in *The Dynamics of Forgiveness,* claims that "realized forgiveness," not obedience as some theologians claim, is central in the Christian faith. By this he means that whatever else is understood about the Christian religion you will not be able to respond effectively or practice it satisfactorily unless you experience forgiveness.

Paul was trying to say that love was central in I Corinthians Thirteen. There is no conflict between Paul's emphasis and Emerson's. Forgiveness is love in action. Love confronts us in the framework of forgiveness because we have broken our relationship with God, and continue to do so; therefore forgiveness is love's road back home to God.

What precisely, then, do we experience as forgiveness? What occurs in the forgiver and in the forgiven? What happens at each end of this polarity experience? Assuming that a relationship has been ruptured, how does forgiveness restore it?

Initially, there must be an acceptance of the fact that either one or both parties have suffered. If both have caused injury, as in many a family quarrel, both must accept the suffering the other has caused. "You have hurt me" need not be the cry of self-pity; it may be a factual statement. The truth may read, "You have lied about me," or "You have caused me sleepless nights." Whatever the offense is, unless the forgiver sees that personal suffering must be borne and accepted, there is no point in confronting the offender with what has happened in the broken relationship.

I am amazed at how both secular psychologists and theologians skip this aspect of forgiveness. Without willingness to acknowledge the piercing pain of what happened and live with it until it has been assimilated there can be no forgiveness. It is like a fever when the body is fighting an infection. The fever is nature's way of working through to health. So is suffering when you have been hurt.

When you have been wounded, you hurt; you bleed inside; you feel the fever of hate and the pains of grief along with ambiguity and confusion of having run smack into a part of life that seems absurd. For example, a certain woman discovered that her husband had been having an affair with a woman at the office. Adding insult to injury he claimed that he could not hurt the other woman by telling her that he was through. It looked as if fifteen years of a reasonably happy marriage was going down the drain. Then, the man came to his senses, declared his love for his wife and children, got the other woman out of his office, and closed the whole issue.

Week after week the wife sat in my office and said, "I can't forgive him. I know that I helped cause it, but I still cannot get over it and give my trust to him again."

At one point I said, "Do you have any idea what the Bible means when it says that Jesus bore our sins in His body on the cross?" She taught a Sunday school class and had often talked about the meaning of the cross. I pointed out that for an effective reconciliation involving a depth relationship, the one sinned against must always suffer, and that she had to get under the burden of his moral failure and help him bear it.

Later she admitted that as she began to see the cross aspect of forgiveness she was able to feel love for her husband again. She said, "I found myself saying that I should feel compassion for him; knowing how he has hurt us must be an awful burden to bear." She abandoned all rage and retaliation and self-pity, and asked him to forgive her for utterly rejecting him in his dark hour.

Another ingredient in forgiveness is finding a rationale.

Jesus said, "Father, forgive them; for they know not what they do" (Luke 23:34).

Joseph said to his brothers who had sold him as a slave into Egypt: "Fear not: for am I in the place of God? But as for you, ye thought evil against me; but God meant it unto good to bring to pass, as it is this day, to save much people alive. Now therefore fear ye not: I will nourish you, and your little ones. And he comforted them and spake kindly unto them" (Gen. 50:19-21, KJV). This is an example of the healthy-souled man who refuses to play God, who finds a rationale for the evil that occurred to him, who actually transcends injury by using it to become strong, and generously tried to keep those who had hurt him from punishing themselves. Few people in history have stood so tall.

Unfortunately, most people have to find reasons and slogans and catch phrases to explain their dilemmas. Here are some of the rationalizations that people who have been hurt use: It was the devil in him. He didn't realize how it would hurt me. He was resentful but has gotten over that now. He was drinking too much. Something happened to him in his childhood that makes him do those things. He is sick. Most of the time he is good and kind.

In working through to forgiveness, people reveal their deeper themes about life, their basic philosophies, and their own feelings about themselves. The "unforgiving legalist," to use Wayne Oates' phrase, goes by the letter of the law and really feels that forgiveness is either weak or sinful. The fatalist will assume "once a sinner always a sinner" in the sense that human nature cannot be changed. This is a dastardly insult to human beings, but determinists breed determinisms. The person who can be free to create and to forgive himself will go about seeing all sorts of situations that call for forgiveness and acceptance. To forgive is human as well as to err.

At this point it should be admitted that forgiveness is not usually a sudden or quickly accomplished state. Just as the bereaved have to do what has been called "the grief work," such as going over and over the good points of the deceased, so the injured have to look at what happened from every angle. This is probably the mind's way of avoiding unnecessary future injuries. The real transition into a state of realized forgiveness occurs when some new perspective (verbalized as a rationale, mentioned above) is achieved.

It may be the professed repentance of the offender. Then again, even a pledge of changed behavior, without any explanation concerning the past, may be the occasion of the forgiving experience. Jesus said that if our brother repents, forgive him even to seventy times seven times (Matt. 18:21-22). His repentance, if it is genuine, gives the forgiver a rationale, and it gives the forgiver a fresh approach to life situations.

Perhaps the most important rationale that any human being involved in estrangement ever achieves is that of acceptance of failure. We have to shake hands with the facts about how limited we as human beings are. Most of us blunder through life hurting those we love and neglecting those who need our love. We cannot expect to get beyond the time when we will not need to forgive and to request forgiveness.

No one can live closely with another human being without

being in a forgiveness situation. Employers have to forgive employees for past failure. Employees, likewise, must forgive employers. Parents have to forgive children for their ingratitude and presumption. Children have to forgive parents for their over-solicitation, arrogance, and unnecessary domination. Husbands and wives have to forgive negligence, ego-sabotaging, and indifference. The list could be extended indefinitely, to church, school, hospital, and even the funeral home.

The late Paul Tillich sees the courage to live with our imperfections, "the courage to accept oneself as accepted in spite of being unacceptable," as rooted in our belief in forgiveness. Without this kind of experience, we would not be able to respond to God. It is accepting the unacceptable. It is a necessary rationale, human nature being what it is.

The climax of all forgiveness, the end results of all movements toward and through the experience of forgiveness, is a good relationship.

It should now be clear that forgiveness does not cancel sin or make us forget or overlook bad behavior. The primary aim of all forgiveness is sound and rich interaction between persons. It is the passion for relatedness that makes forgiveness so important. This does not mean, of course, that because we know God in a forgiveness-trusting relationship that we will be soundly related to all people. If we think for a moment that people under all circumstances will forgive us if we repent, or that all who offend wish to be forgiven, we are childishly naïve. As greatly as forgiveness is needed in this world, it is not likely to be practiced on a wide scale in the foreseeable future.

Anders Nygren, the Swedish theologian, related the following story. A modern youth had tried to live out the parable of the Prodigal Son. The prodigality, squandering, and sinning he did well. Then he decided to leave his wicked friends and return to the father. A few days later when he saw his former companions they asked, "Well, did your father kill the fatted calf for you?" "No," replied the youth, "but he almost killed the prodigal son."

The Christian approach to the situations that call for forgiveness includes three things: (1) honestly attempting to avoid offenses that tax relationships; (2) admitting of our faults and our failures once they are observed by us; and (3) maintaining a constant, aggressive readiness to forgive.

The first two of these have often been talked about a great deal, but the readiness to forgive is often winked at. Jesus indicated that a prerequisite to worship was reconciliation with "your brother" (Matt. 5:23-24). The task of the church involves relationship rebuilding (Matt. 18:15-20). Throughout the New Testament we see a readiness to forgive and aggressive attempts at enriching relationships emphasized. To the Romans, Paul wrote, "Never pay back evil for evil. . . . My dear friends," do not seek revenge, but leave a place for divine retribution (Rom. 12:17, 19, NEB). He urged the Ephesians not to let the sun go down on their anger but to forgive one another as God in Christ had forgiven them (Eph. 4:26-32).

In all the ways possible, with all the individuals possible, and in all the circumstances possible, we are to be all forgiving; and this from our hearts.

CHAPTER 8

Love Is A Many-Splendored Thing

Love Is A Many Splendored Thing—this is the way millions of people experience love. It is the April rose that only grows in the early spring, two lovers kissing in the morning mist. Yes, throughout the centuries millions of people have expressed love in sentimental overtones.

But to countless others love is a "strange bewilderment that overtakes one person regarding another person" (James Thurber); or they say with Dorothy Parker, "Love is a permanent flop." In fact, suicide prevention centers offer data indicating that more than half of the people who try to shuck off life do so because of matters relating to love. And not a few homicides revolve around this great theme.

For the moment let us set aside aspects of love which might predominantly involve sex, infatuation, romance, selfishness, possession, and narcissism. There must be more mature relationships which are not merely intellectual, spiritual, or platonic, but which are down-to-earth, splendored, and give us profound reasons for living.

I like the words of Robert Frost in his poem, "The Birches:"

> Earth's the right place for love.
> I don't know where it's likely to go better.

Here are some creative definitions of love given to us by some of the world's greatest thinkers. These certainly sound down-to-earth and practical.

Emil Brunner writes of love as the unconditional will to community; it has no limits and makes no conditions. Paul Johnson defines love as growing interest in, appreciation of, and responsibility for, every person. Paul Tillich says that love is the drive towards the unity of the separated, and that reunion presupposes the separation of that which essentially belongs together. Rollo May defines love as a delight in the presence of another person and an affirmation of his value and development as much as one's own. The late Harry Stack Sullivan said that love exists when the satisfaction and security of another person becomes as significant to one as one's own satisfaction and security.

Love, as these definitions suggest, is something that occurs between persons. Interpersonal reaction, positive, construc tive, health-giving response to another. In the case of God's love to us, it is life-giving. It involves seeing the person in a favorable manner. It involves feelings and actions, always. Love is an energy to be expended, not a vacuum to be filled. Love is the warm acceptance of and communion with another person as he is and as a whole.

Even in accepting this definition, we must admit to its inadequacy. *Communion* must involve more than verbal communion. Surely there are times when love's greatest feel ing is expressed in silence. And *warm* might be construed to mean mushy or possessive or smothering. To accept a person as a whole may involve tolerating without protest his filth, or alcoholism, or untreated mental illness. Yet I must generally commit myself to the warm acceptance of and communion with another person as he is and as a whole. If I qualify this definition at times, it is but testimony to the admitted complexity of human life.

But defining love is not as important as recognizing it when we see it. A famous poet said, "I cannot define a poem any more than a cat can define a rat, but recognize one when he sees it." To recognize love, in God, in ourselves, or in others, is to be able to respond to a loving act. To act sincerely in a loving manner is to love. These loving acts and patterns of love are largely, if not solely, *learned* by the human being. We learn from our teachers. Have you ever noticed that a little child, when faced with a puzzling situation, quickly glances at his mother's or father's face? It is his first significant response to novelty. From them and their response he will get his cue as to his own appropriate response.

Is it not possible that this is how we learn to love? See where God is looking and focus our attention there. May not success result in finding out what God is doing in the world and joining forces with Him? "Looking unto Jesus the pioneer and perfecter of our faith" is the way the writer of Hebrews worded it (12:2). Paul in II Corinthians speaks of "the light of the knowledge of the glory of God in the face of Jesus Christ" (4:6).

Love as God loved, is the message of the whole New Testament, especially of the Gospel and the Epistles of John. And Jesus said, "This is my commandment, that you love one another as I have loved you" (John 15:12). It sounds as if He is saying that this one commandment summarizes all of the other commandments, or that this one must stand out and be emphasized above everything else. Again, the Apostle John wrote some very striking statements about the importance of love, in his first Epistle, Chapter 4: "For God is love; and his love was disclosed to us in this, that he sent his only Son into the world to bring us life . . . If God thus loved us, dear friends, we in turn are bound to love one another . . . We love because he loved us first . . . And indeed this command comes to us from Christ himself: that he who loves God must also love his brother."

Now, how does the fact that we love God fit into our definition of acceptance and communion? It fits perfectly. To keep this greatest of all commandments, to love God with all that is within us means to accept God as God and address Him and listen to Him as God. Therefore, to love God will involve work (keeping His commandments), worship, praise, prayer, adoration, trust, and listening.

At this point in our thinking, it will be helpful to consider the answers to these questions. How does God's love work? What does it do? How does a loving God act? What is the constant process of Divine love?

God's love is universal. He loves everyone everywhere. This sends our imagination reeling. Actually, in a limited way we may find it possible to accept this concept and acknowledge its truth, but unfortunately, we are not "good enough" to put it into practice. It is so much easier to sing of His loving the whole world than for us to love each person with whom we come in contact.

Most of us can love and accept those who are like us, have the same set of values, the same mores, and especially the same folkways. We love our families, although at times this seems to impose a bit of a strain. And usually we find it fairly easy to love those of our own particular faith, social class, and race.

But the test of real love is loving those who present some kind of problem or threat to us. Labels can be dangerous. The emotional, lecherous Nigger, the lazy Red Skin, the conniving Jew, the impulsive Dago, the homosexual, the feeble-minded, the insane—see what these labels do for us! They put a film over our eyes. We label our fellows and then we react to them as labeled. Labels are devices used by talkative people to save them the trouble of thinking, and of loving.

Loving an individual—wife, five-year-old son, aged grandparent, employer, gossipy neighbor or janitor—begins with seeing him a certain way. As a person, not as a thing. But to love is more than seeing; it is openness to all the person's varied, hidden, deformed, and dwarfed qualities.

"Love the sinner but hate his sin" has become a threadbare and deceptive slogan behind which religious people have often hidden. There is no sinner apart from the sins which are engrained in his makeup, and no sins apart from sinners. If we mean, "When I confront the sinner, I love him so much that I wish he did not possess these sins," that is a different matter. It may even be necessary to confine the sinner to keep him from destroying others, since he persists in being recalcitrant. Perhaps this is the meaning of the Bible concept of hell. William Booth said, "Preach hell with the cross right in its center."

God's love is continuous, indiscriminate, unprejudiced and without exception. To use Franklin D. Roosevelt's expression, there are no "forgotten men." Not with God. But there are "forgotten men" in our lives—in our cities, our schools, our governments, our world, and even in our churches.

The life-giving blessing of sunshine and rain are given equally to the "just and the unjust," Jesus said, and are constant broadcasts of God's continuous love (Matt. 5:43-48). How comfortable we all feel with this thought. God has no fences around His love, no boundary lines, no snake pits where His presence is not intruded.

> He drew a circle that shut me out—
> Heretic, rebel, a thing to flout.
> But Love and I had the wit to win!
> We drew a circle that took him in!
> —EDWIN MARKHAM[1]

Loving would not be so difficult if we could adopt the profound viewpoint which is suggested by the definition of Emil Brunner's: *God's love has no limits and no conditions.* So often, though, we violate God's inclusiveness and impose limits and conditions to our love. At one time or another most of us have said, "I could love him if he were lovely." But it is at this very point that divine love transcends our human love. The loveableness of the other person is not to be the cause of our love. Like God's love, Christian love is spontaneous, uncaused, and unexplained. The only "limit" to God's love is in its reception. And love, both human and divine, must be received by faith.

With this admitted exception then, how do we see God's love overcoming limits that other love possesses?

Man's love says, "I will love you until . . ." The *until* may be until you disappoint me, until I find out the truth about you, until you stub your toe morally, until you disagree with me, until you hurt me or my friend or relative, until you

[1]Edwin Markham, "Outwitted."—Reprinted by permission of Virgil Markham.

change (as all people do change as they go through life), until I find out that you hate me.

Dr. Martin Luther King has an eloquent message for forgiveness, which is a necessary component of love when it confronts failure and limitation:

> Ask an innocent young lady, who, after a moment of overriding passion, becomes the mother of an illegitimate child. She will tell you that society is slow to forgive. Ask public official, who, in a moment's carelessness, betrays the public trust. He will tell you that society is slow to forgive. Go to any prison and ask the inhabitants, who have written shameful lines across the pages of their lives. From behind bars, they will tell you that society is slow to forgive. Make your way to death row and speak with the tragic victims of criminality. As they prepare to make their pathetic walk to the electric chair, their hopeless cry is that society will not forgive. Capital punishment is society's final assertion that it will not forgive.[2]

I am not claiming here that love can redeem and reform *all* mankind. So far in the history of the world, this seems to be merely a fantastic dream. But like the attempt to equate forgiving with forgetting, we have often neutralized the power of love by refusing love to those whom we once alleged to have loved but they have disappointed us. Now we do not love them. Did we ever? Is love truly Christian which alters when it alteration finds?

Love is unconditional in that it never loves *if* . . . . if I could get you to respond on my terms, if your skin were a different color, if we believed the same things about God, if you were not a Communist, if you will promise never to

[2]Martin Luther King. *Strength To Love,* (New York: Harper and Row, Inc., 1963), p. 33.

repeat your mistake again, if you will be grateful for my love these "ifs" trouble our sleep because we know that if there is no greater love than this limited kind, we are in grave danger. How can any of us be safe in a universe where the Ultimate Reality says, "I will love you if . . . .?"

This poses an important theological and ethical problem for Christians. Are justice and righteousness not related to love? Is God like the unwise and doting parents, or grandparents, who leave the impression with the child that he can do anything he likes and still be accepted? I think not.

The solution seems to be in the power of God's graciousness. If it is truly received the one loved identifies, more or less, with the one extending love. If we devour love and make no attempt at responsibility, we have not entered into the meaning of love.

This sounds like I am saying, "I will love you if you will enter into the meaning of love and become a responsible person." This is not quite accurate. Rather I am saying that there is a polarity to love. If it is not received, it has no meaning. To love *at* a person is largely meaningless. To illustrate, if a person does not respond to God's love or to man's, it is like dialing the number of a person who is sitting right by the phone on the other end of the line, but refuses to pick up the receiver and take the call. Receptivity and person-response is the only condition God places on his love. Even this does not preclude His readiness to love or His attempting to show his love. This very idea appalls me, and inspires me.

Another facet of conditional love is that man loves *because* . . . . God loves differently. We act on a love that if expressed clearly would read: "I love you because you are my child, or my customer, or my childhood friend." God does not love us because He sees our potential or because we have not failed Him—nor *because* of anything. No, the essence of Christian love is stated in the prepositional phrase, *in spite of*. God loves us in spite of our sins, our ingratitude, our coldness, our stupidity, our immaturity—the list can be extended to all the vagaries of human nature or the vicissitudes of life.

Perhaps the most astounding aspect of God's love is its *impartiality*. In a world of caste systems, false values, competition, and jealousy, we do not find it easy to accept ourselves as the direct and indiscriminate object of God's loving. Similarly, we find it difficult to accept man as God gives him to us, as we happen to confront him.

Most of us could believe that God's love is extended to Schweitzer, Einstein, Salk, Beethoven, or perhaps to soldiers in battle, or to presidents, kings, and legislators. With them so much was and is at stake. It comes easy for us to see God as sponsor of the producers, the creators, and of the researchers. But listen to Simon Peter after he had been stabbed wide awake by a dream-trance. He was commanded to eat that which was not kosher. Out of this shock-teaching came a new concept of man, stated by Simon very clearly when he arrived at the home of the Gentile, Roman army officer: "God has shown me that I should not call any man common or unclean" (Acts 10:28). "God shows no partiality" was Peter's succinct summary of his object lesson. He moved into a new dimension of Christian living, preaching and emphasis. He saw that God had no pets, played no favorites. The application of Christ's life and message broke out of traditional territories.

James, in his Epistle, applied this new principle of "no favorites" to behavior around church meetings. He says that if rich people attend church and you give them the favorite seats, while poor people are treated as inferiors, you sin. "Show no partiality" he boldly commands, and then says that to show partiality is a sin against God (James 2:1-13). Strangely enough he invokes one of the best-known statements in the Old and New Testaments, calling it *the royal law*, "You shall love your neighbor as yourself" (2:8). To show partiality is a flagrant violation of this verse.

"Thy neighbor as thyself." We have heard the words from infancy. It is a phrase brimful of possible meanings. Unless you love yourself, and see that God loves you as you are, as much as and the same as He loves every other one of His creatures, you cannot love the one near you (your neighbor).

On the other hand it may mean that you are to love your neighbor as one like yourself. He fears, hungers, hates and loves, like you do. He longs to be accepted in all of his uniqueness—just like you do. He needs to have communion with his fellow-man, the same as you do.

It certainly means that you are to love your fellow-man the same as, and while you are loving, yourself—neither more nor less. The self-inflicting person loves others more, or tries to, than himself. The selfish person loves himself extravagantly, and loves others only if they will love him in return or to the extent that they are useful to him.

Instead of pursuing the idea of impartiality further, let me say that it is my firm opinion that no one has ever really practiced this and the other aspects of love, except God in Jesus Christ. This is an example of the very nature of an ideal.

In our homes we all grew up in a milieu of rejection-acceptance, condition-unconditioned, and partial-impartial responses. We experience this social climate in all of our interpersonal relationships.

What is to be our response to these things? Let's face the

fact that our world is filled with hate, not love. The two are strangely and sadly mixed. Other people want you to warmly accept them, but they either will not or cannot return the same. This is one honest approach.

But faith responds differently. It says that since there is so little love in the world, let me throw my weight on the side of loving, even as God loves me. "We love because he loved us first," John said. We cannot give love until we receive it. But once it is received it can be given naturally. Yet, apparently, we need to be urged to practice it. So God calls us to be like Him—as like Him as we can by His grace.

A Bedouin invited a guest to spend the night with him. After the evening meal he asked his stranger-guest, "Who is your God?" "I have no god," was the simple reply, "I am an atheist." Whereupon the Bedouin drove him out of his tent into the night. In his troubled dreams that night God seemed to say to him: "Come out into the night and look at the beautifully spangled tent I have stretched over your head and over the heads of all my creatures. Could you not allow this stranger, who doesn't know as much as he might know about Me, to stay under your tent for one night?"

In the words of Frost again:

> Earth's the right place for love.
> I don't know where it's likely to go better.

Or in the words of Jesus: "This is my commandment, that you love one another as I have loved you." Truly love is many splendored!

CHAPTER 9

The Three Temptations of Mankind

It is so easy to read the Bible without seeing that it deals with the very problems we are facing.

There are really three ways to read a particular section. We can take it to pieces, analyze it, turn each archaic stone over until we understand all of its museum potentialities— this is called exegesis. Or we may look at the great ideas in a passage in the light of the whole book or letter, or even in the light of the total philosophy of the author and the times. This is called exposition. It is more like a tourist who looks at all the curios of particular historical interest and goes on his way supplied with more conversational material.

Exegesis and exposition may end in paralysis and exhibitionism with no deep pertinence to my inner life. They may leave me untouched and unspoken to. The Scriptures connect with my own experience only if they are from the heart of men who have touched essentially the same facets of life which I have touched, and have reacted to them in a way that speaks to me.

Such, I believe, is the account of the temptations of Jesus. It speaks to my situation, to something within me that is universal, though colored by our cultural or social milieus. For years, I have read the three temptations of Jesus when He "was led by the Spirit into the wilderness to be tempted by the devil" (Matt. 4:1) with a satisfied certainty. The first one—"command these stones to become loaves of bread" —meant that the Master was tempted to succumb to the lusts and hungers of the flesh: sex, drink, and food. The second, about leaping from the pinnacle of the temple, was the urge to turn religion into magic, into the spectacular. The third temptation, involving "all the kingdoms of the world and the glory of them," was the invitation to achieve a good end by bad means. The means justify the ends, many think. These were my thoughts on the temptations of Jesus.

Such moral lessons are not without application to our social situation. They are, however, largely conclusions made by man as he looked at his fellow man. We see man devouring things to his detriment, making religion a pageant of the sensational, and dazzled by the delight of conquest.

An even further method of avoiding the relevance of the temptation story is to say, "We must remember that this was the Son of God who was being tested in the wilderness. Satan began the temptation with the words, 'If you are the Son of God?' (Matt. 4:3) To descend from the pinnacle of the temple and have the angels of God swoop down under him in order to avoid a smash-up would certainly convince the multitudes. And, after all, concerning the last temptation, the purpose of the Advent and the Resurrection of Christ was to become king of kings, to gain the kingdoms of the world—whatever that means!" Such a high-flown interpretation is a precise example of hiding truth rather than applying it. It says that this story is a beautiful example of how Jesus met temptations, and it has little pertinence to our experiences because we are not "the sons of God."

Let me suggest that we lay aside our Bible commentaries, ignore the explanatory footnotes, forget the sermons we have heard on the subject of temptation, and ask ourselves, "Where does this story of Christ's tests (the literal meaning of temptation) apply to me? Not how, but where?"

John Ciardi, the modern poet and teacher, says of the people of Milan, Italy: "The Milanese do not study opera, they inhale it."[1] This may be the way to study the Bible. As we read the accounts of the temptation in Matthew 4, Mark 1, or Luke 4, how does it become a part of us? Obviously, something keeps us from absorbing and experiencing this story, if my own past interpretations are typical. If commentaries and books on the life of Christ are good examples of the interpretations of the temptations, there is meaning to our blindness. We are tempted to obscure the problems which Christ faced in order to avoid the challenge to face up to what is wrong in our lives.

Let us stand before the facts with an open mind.

A young Gallilean peasant had become aware of (or deluded into believing) the fact that He was the special agent of God here to reveal salvation to man. To achieve His unique being He felt led to go aside from the routines of life and think, and think; and feel, and feel. Fasting, living on juices or completely without solid food, He had achieved a special victory in spiritual matters. He tried it alone, all alone, for forty days. There were moments of ecstacy. This brought a distinctiveness and a feeling of being special.

[1] *How Does a Poem Mean?* (Boston: Houghton Mifflin Company, 1959), p. 666.

At a particular point a voice may have said, "Stay here. Do not return to those grimy, mixed-up people. Turn this stone (which, no doubt, looked like a baked piece of bread) into bread, and you can avoid returning to the problems and perplexities of human nature. Turn away from life, from people, from need, from suffering, from involvement. Turn away. Don't go back into the demands and expectations of relatedness. You can be apart, aloof, separate, detached. All you will have to do is turn this stone into bread."

His reply was, to paraphrase it, "Man cannot exist on material things; he needs relationships." Jesus' statement, "every word that proceeds from the mouth of God," we can see, is a way of affirming that we are primarily creatures of response and that things cannot suffice.

A delinquent, who was incarcerated in a state correctional institution for stealing bicycles, said to his therapist at a particular juncture in their conversations, "I see now that I wanted love. I did not feel that I got it from my parents, so I took things. Now, I see that things cannot love me back. I must give my love to people who can love me back."

There are many ways to flee from relationships. Turning away, refusing to be close to anyone is as common as sunshine and as destructive as wind. The business man often turns away from his family, even brings unnecessary work home from the office, in order to have an excuse for not facing his family in intimacy and warmth. The wife often flees to the children or to the bridge game to keep from confessing her emptiness and her fear of closeness. The teenager runs and runs, and talks and talks on the telephone in order to avoid the realization that he is afraid of life. He flees from reality. Many superficial relationships preclude other more significant relationships of frankness, openness, and depth. The older person gets quieter and quieter and more perfunctory in order to hide his fear of old age and death. We flee into recreation, religion, drink, tranquillizers, and LSD in order to avoid the transparency and frankness and natural communication that normal life affords.

The second temptation[2] is the tendency to show off or get attention in improper ways.

Christ's reply to Satan gives the clue. "You shall not tempt the Lord your God." The gist is: don't be constantly putting God to a test. Live within His constructed reality. Don't allow yourself to expect Him to do handsprings for you. Jesus must have spoken with a tone of sorrow and hurt when He said to the father who sought a miracle of healing for his sick son, "Unless you see signs and wonders, you will not believe." (John 4:48).

Why would this test God? For the very reason that He does make promises and offer help, but on His terms. Or to be more precise, God acts according to His own wisdom, and when we make demands which grow out of our immature needs, we complicate the relationship. It is a kind of putting God on the spot. This must never be. It is as if we say, "Look, Father, You have promised to be good to me, and this is the way I interpret goodness. Come across."

Now we begin to sense the thrust of the pinnacle temptation. Jesus had to get attention in order to influence people. Furthermore, His unique ministry was not only to get attention but to demonstrate the power of God in the extremes of human living as well as in the routines of daily grinds.

---

[2]We follow Matthew's account rather than Luke's for the simple reason that the appeal to the Christ to possess the kingdoms of the earth, as well as our own lust for power, seems more of a climax to the temptations.

Who does not wish significance? Who does not wish to be distinctive, perhaps even distinguished? Who does not ask himself how he looks in the eyes of others? Can self-evaluation ever completely divorce itself from reputation?

A sense of selfhood so easily moves over into fearing the faces of others who are proximate to the self, or into compromises and playing roles which are aimed at securing us in the esteem of significant others.

Wherein, then, lies the heart of this temptation? In two facets of human struggling: the false means we use to get significance; and in the passive, unrealistic attempts to get God or angels or even friends to take care of us. "He will give his angels charge of you" and "they will bear you up."

We do all sorts of things to get attention, we get sick and force those about us to listen to our complaints. Of course, this does not mean that all sickness is emotionally caused. It is a fact, though, as any physician can verify, that many illnesses are serving the purpose of getting some kind of ego satisfactions. Many persons cannot get well and stay well until they learn to tolerate the normal frustration of not being loved as they wish they were.

We get attention, too, by getting our feelings hurt when we are not honored, respected, admired, appreciated. Who has not been tempted to quit doing for others because they do not appreciate it? Cynicism over the sharp-toothed ingratitude close to us has instigated many a resignation, even in the churches.

Another attention getter is plain, unabashed upstaging. This occurs in every group from time to time. In kindergarten kids fight to be at the head of the line. In the big business firms, the kindergartner's grandfather may resort to foul play, character assassination, or social bribery to become a vice-president. The kindergartner's father is trying to win a trip to Hawaii or to Las Vegas by outselling others in his company. Or perhaps the father is neglecting to pay his honest doctor's bill because he has bought a new boat to keep up with the Joneses.

It would seem that the crux of this temptation is not that we should reduce our desires to zero, but that we should not cultivate exorbitant expectations in what we expect from people. Nor should we use evil or offensive or destructive means of getting ahead. In short, that we must not expect either man or God to cater to our egotistic longings.

Prayer can be a perfect illustration of this temptation. Privately, we may expect God to make us His pets and protect us from all hardships, or we may demand that He suddenly produce mature characters in us without the suffering and struggle and perplexity that others have faced.

Public prayers have often been addressed to the audience. It seems to meet a wider variety of our human needs if we can appear both clever and Christian at the same time. There is double-entendre in much of our piety.

This second temptation almost invariably is based upon an assumption that somebody ought to take care of us. We have many needs which only God and others can meet. And given the right conditions, God and others will come across. Often we do not even know what those conditions are. Distrust may thwart our opening to God and man. Our common dictum, not in the Bible and not even a Scriptural idea, says that "God helps those who help themselves." This makes a good alibi for unbelief or for not approaching God for help. However, back of this proverb is the realization that you cannot passively expect God to do for you what you should do for yourself; and you cannot defy the laws of gravity, for example, and expect Him to "bear you up." He will have to let you down unless you consult with His real world, physical as well as moral and spiritual.

The third temptation defines itself more easily, but the viciousness of the patterns of behavior involved are hard to face when they are *our* patterns or patterns of those close around us. We develop rationalizations that blind our eyes and befog our minds so that our own power struggles appear noble and useful and healthy. This temptation is that of controlling or getting power over others. *The will to power.* This, like the other two, is not alien to the normal, inherent nature of man. We need solitariness and recognition. Likewise we certainly need at times to control and manipulate the environment, including other people.

Where does one draw the line? When does natural ambition move across the line into inordinate thirst for power? When is a talk salesmanship and when is it teaching? What is the distinction between leadership and dictatorship (or propaganda, for that matter)? Even in controlling our children, how do we distinguish between making threats and describing consequences?

We do not have to look any farther than our children's play room or our grandparents' sun porch to see that the struggle between human beings to control one another is persistent and perpetual. Most of the unhappiness and cruelty of the world grows out of the fact that one human being is trying to dominate or coerce others.

The infant must be subjected to control. This will be resisted when the controls are at cross purposes with his desires, but unfortunately, just about the time he matures to the point of being able to control himself (whenever that is), some adult (one or more) presumes to subjugate him and keep him under his direction. This may be achieved by making him feel guilty, threatening to withdraw love or to harm him physically or socially, appealing to his pity, or even by alleging that God or man will reject or punish him.

On the other hand, no one in his right mind would argue for a random, uncontrolled world. Either we control ourselves or someone else must control us. Religion and most forms of democracy unite in affirming that every person should be given as much freedom as his responsibility and the social situation will allow. However, every student of history recognizes the existence of forces in every age that seek to inherit and to enfold unwary mankind in their bind. Enslavement is a constant social, spiritual, and political hazard.

The child moves out of his primary groups—the home and the school—and discovers that in every cluster of people there are those who are bumping into each other, shoving killing, robbing, commanding, and vieing for power. Even the animal world has its hierarchies and control systems which are highly reflective of what man does. A reputable group of social and natural history scientists insist that man and the higher primates seem never to escape some natural tendencies deep within them. They refer to territoriality and the need to dominate.[3]

The gist of this theory is that there is an inherent desire to dominate and a tendency to stake out our territories that lies so deep in nature, especially human, that it is a "romantic fallacy" (Ardrey's term) to think that we can overcome it

[3]Those wishing to see more elaborate discussions of these concepts may consult Robert Ardrey's *African Genesis* (New York: Dell Publishing Company, 1961); Roger Brown's *Social Psychology* (New York: The Free Press, 1965); or V. C. Wynne-Edwards' *Animal Dispersion in Relation to Social Behavior* (Edinburgh and London: Oliver and Boyd, 1962).

by a new economic order or by the welfare state. Men form themselves into groups, decide who their enemies are, establish boundaries, tyrannize both their enemies and the subordinates of their own group. Neither food nor sex is the primary drive, but territoriality lies at the base of our human problems.

A professor at the University of Aberdeen (Wynne-Edwards), a Yale psychologist (Roger Brown), and an American playright (Ardrey), in their discussions of territoriality, underline a truth that Jesus touched on many times, "Forgive us our trespasses as we forgive those who trespass against us." This phrase in the Lord's Prayer is based firmly on territoriality.

Jesus said, "You know that in the world, rulers lord it over their subjects and their great men make them feel the weight of authority; but it shall not be so with you" (Matt. 20:25 NEB). The greatest were to be those who served most. But unfortunately, this has not been the pattern, even in the churches. There may even be those who would feel that Jesus was not realistic in making this particular statement; that no society can survive without its kings, its king-makers, its image creators whose primary purpose is the manipulating of the minds of men. It would appear that no church, with the possible exception of the Quakers, has survived merely by witnessing. Churches which have grown large in numbers have been powerful through the use of power structures and power techniques. On a large scale, no religious group in the world has had faith enough to resist the temptation to throw-its-weight, to enjoy the power it acquires. This may be the next significant movement in the religious world—growth by the use of spiritual rather than temporal power.

Jesus resisted the temptation to play God. His succinct reply to Satan was, "You shall worship the Lord your God and him only shall you serve" (Matt. 4:10). "Let God be God!" seems to be what He was saying. Then too, He presented another side of this "God complex" when He warned the disciples against being called "master" or "rabbi," saying that they were all to be brothers. He said to call no one on earth your father "for you have one Father, who is in heaven" (Matt. 23:9). Similarly, the Apostle Paul warned, that Christians are not to punish one another in revenge (Romans 12:19-21), or to pass judgment on one another's goodness or badness (Romans 14:10-18) because both of these prerogatives belong to God.

The widespread applications of this temptation are so numerous that they stagger us. Much attempt to convert or help save another has been but an attempt to rule over the other. Businessmen work themselves into an early grave in their drive for control. Husbands and wives battle to the destruction of their own happiness and the emotional illness of their children to keep from being "run over". The battle of the sexes has often led to the defeat of people who otherwise might have been saints.

This temptation has enveloped all mankind. Whether we rule from our sick bed by making people wait on us out of sympathy, or rage in a threatening tone of voice to get our own way, or talk and pray another person into complying with our wishes, we are ingenious in our techniques of tyranny.

Jesus, the Son of God and son of man, was tempted in every respect as we are yet without sinning (Heb. 4:15). He was "lured and enticed by his own desire" (James 1:14) to turn away, to show off, to dominate, and yet He found the strength to resist. How did He do it? He remained alert, never denying His relatedness. Bread alone (things for the stomach or ideas for the mind) will not take the place of communication—"every word that proceeds from the mouth of God." Consequently, He could not stay in the wilderness, away from man.

Jesus refused to play a false role. Imagine Him crushed and broken on the pavement below the watch tower of the temple as someone says, "He expected too much of life. He acted as if he was God's pet and would not have to suffer the same laws that control others. He tried to be distinctive the wrong way." Many a man has played a false role at the pinnacle of his career—not Jesus.

Jesus withstood temptation because "He never forgot who He was." And, we too might keep from falling into perverse relationships with God or man if "we would not forget who we are."

CHAPTER 10

For Those Who Believe That They Believe

For many years, I have been puzzled by one remark that Jesus made. "The sons of this world are wiser in their own generation than the sons of light" (Luke 16:8). Even the New English Bible does not help much, except to sting us deeper: "For the worldly are more astute than the otherworldly in dealing with their own kind." Is it possible He is saying that the world is smarter than the church? Use your heads. Let common sense be your guide. Consecrate common sense. Think. Use your heads!

To one observer, at least, the church needs to get smart. This sounds like an appropriate word for the modern church. Our failures have been flagrant. Try as we may, we cannot hide the fact that in a day when business has been enterprising and successful the church has been apologetic and failing. Greater numbers have not brought greater power or deeper insights. Even greater numbers are deceptive. In the last fifty years, Communism has grown at a much greater rate than Christianity, but numbers, do not necessarily measure strength. There are much more subtle and important factors, such as commitment, confidence in our cause, hope, and the image of where we are going.

The secular world has its shrewd tactics, as illustrated in the parable which precedes this very astute remark of Jesus. It relies upon image creation, upon sales promotion, upon lobbying, upon threat of punishment, upon rewards for conforming behavior, and even upon brainwashing and barnstorming. However, Jesus said that we were to operate on a different plane. In Luke 22, and parallel passages, He said that in the world they "lord it over their subjects"—throw their weight around—and call those in authority "benefactors." This is not the Christian way. We are to become great by becoming small, to rise by kneeling, to stand tall by stooping to help, to soar by serving. What a surprising attack on the problem of finding meaning!

A look at today's church reveals that too frequently we have adopted the world's criteria: numbers, power, crowds, money, buildings. Many ministers feel that if they do not show results in converts, in building, in church budget, in contributions to denominational causes, they will fail to be promoted. After all, these are the things that show up in the annual reports? How can we measure spiritual progress except by numbers and material gains? Jesus would answer, "Forget the measuring and bear witness. I will attend to the outcome."

It must be admitted, however, that we do not know what Jesus would say to the churches if He were here. Yet we cannot be true to ourselves unless we turn the searchlight of His Word toward every area of our lives. Try as we may, we cannot avoid what psychologists call "selective attention." We attend to certain truths and overlook others. We pick out what we want to see, the cynic might say. This is hardly true. Rather, we *hear* that part of the Word of God which speaks particularly to our needs and to the stresses of our times. Actually, what we *see* in the Bible is determined not merely by what is on the pages but by what is in our own anxious hearts. We see things not as they are but as we are. We read those selections from the Scriptures which speak to our openness.

Today, we find ourselves moving rapidly through the second half of the twentieth century. We are not at all sure where the institutional church is going. Our need of God is still with us, but our hope in Him as the solution to our problems seems to be weakening. Revolutions are occurring all around us—race relations, sex, automation, church union, and statism, to mention only a few areas of rapid change. Trying to describe our times is like an artist taking out his pencil to sketch a horse, and before he completes the main lines, the horse has dashed out of sight.

In the words and format of Don Adams, star of the TV "Get Smart" show, "Would you believe" that Christianity is experiencing the greatest revival and forward movement since the first century? No? Then, "would you believe" that we are holding our own and, at least, growing as fast as Communism? No! "Would you believe that we might be able to do something about our failing situation? Yes.

It is time for us to take a close look at some of our defects—do some healthy self-appraisal. This does not mean that we should become spiritual masochists, indulging in and enjoying self-infliction. Rather, we need to take stock of ourselves for the sake of improvement. And one good place to start would be with our vocabulary. The church is failing to communicate with the world. Ministers and teachers are using words, concepts, and images which are about as pertinent to modern man as the spinning wheel and the surrey with the fringe on top. In a world controlled by democratic assemblies, parliaments, congresses who can warm up to the idea of King of kings and Lord of lords, or even Prince of Peace? What does *redemption* mean in our culture which has barely heard of being sold for our debts and knows slavery only as a lesson in a history book? Redemption to the man in the street or the girl in the office has the connotation of getting some gadget for so many trading stamps. *Grace* is a girl's name, whether blond, brunette or red head, and hardly carries the meaning of gracious behavior. And what does sin mean to the average person? It is loaded, almost exclusively, with prohibitive concepts such as "thou shalt not lie, steal, have bad thoughts, or even smoke, drink, or cuss." Such terms as sanctification, justification, and atonement are complete enigmas to the average Christian and belong along side the discussion of how many angels can stand on the point of a needle.

No, religion is to be relevant—a fight word with some critics of change who think that the question of relevancy is irrelevant—we must interpret it in terms of the characteristic sciences of our times, psychology, and communication. This is not only possible, but plausible. Faith is one personality meeting the *loving other* in openness and expectation of acceptance. Repentance is the peeling off of the facades of pretence concerning our own omniscience and omnipotence. Love is confronting another with willingness to affirm his uniqueness and to receiving him in spite of certain problem traits. Faith, repentance, love—key words in the Christian message—are descriptions of interaction, interpersonal relations.

Christianity has always concerned itself with finding a better way of existing on this earth, not just physically nor economically, but as persons with persons. It involves becoming self-conscious, in the best sense of the word, and asking ourselves what we can become and what will become of us. In searching for answers we may be driven to more primary questions: Who am I? Where did I come from? What is God like, if there is one? What is my relationship to my fellowmen? And, to what is worthy of my time and attention?

Charles Habib Malik, formerly President of the General Assembly of the United Nations, now Distinguished Professor of Philosophy at the American University of Beirut, writes in an article about the Great Society:

> We need to return to earth and nature. We need touch and sight and direct contact. We need to develop a horror of the abstract, a passion for the intimate and concrete. We need gentleness and consideration, patience and understanding, obedience and fidelity, friendship and love. We need the warmth of unity and family love. . . .We need spontaneity and freedom, naturalness and creativity, poetry and vision, peace and rest, the richness of personality and the humility of the person, working toward a transcendent end. We need the detachment of love, the blessedness of the art of listening, the intensity and reality of spiritual experience, the joy of being.

> We need quiet and contemplation, the radiance of saints, the grace of self-giving. We need rootedness in history.

Later in the article he calls for "an authentic voice that will move all men of good will to their deepest depths." Such a man, he says, will be full of fun and full of humanity, one who will point them to the Eternal and cause them to forget themselves. "Such voices cannot be planned or contrived: they are gifts from above."[1] It is unlikely that "an authentic voice" will be sounded from some apartment roof. There may be many voices that have a ring of authenticity, and together they may form a chorus which may stem the tides of destruction.

Without question, the critics of the church can point to much that is wrong—to many instances where it has been far less astute than the "world." Yes, the church is fair game for its critics. But, an equally pertinent question is: what is good about the church? What is close to centralism in the Christian faith? How can we join hearts and lips to extend the growing edge of Christian horizons today? The Beatles may think that they are more popular than Jesus and Margaret Mead may speak of "that tired old thing called the church," but there is evidence of new life all about us. Without getting defensive toward our critics, and without being presumptuous about our ability to distinguish clearly between the trees and the forest, it will serve us well to take a look at the church's distinctive genius.

The power of the church is spiritual. This sounds like another cliché. What we mean is that the strength of religion is in a quality we might define as *inwardness*. It is something inside man that constitutes his glory, as the Christian faith sees him—something that we express in everyday language as courage, attitude, goodwill, love, trust, and concern. Psychologists are dealing with spirit, too. They use these same terms along with others, such as integration, self-actualizing, maturity and wholeness.

[1]Charles Habib Malik, "Reflections on the Great Society," *Saturday Review*, (August 6, 1966), pp. 12-15.

Faith not only deals with inwardness but forces man into a kind of self-awareness which finds pleasure and importance in the spiritual. To be right inside becomes primary. It cannot consider "being right" apart from involvement in and openness to our environment. We look to God and find Him looking at our fellow man. This deflects our attention to ourselves, especially our needy neighbors, but it does not distract us from self or from God.

The focus, then, of the church is on ourselves as spiritual beings, as persons. To talk about our inwardness we have to resort to such terms as imagination, mind, soul, spirit, even will and conscience, as if these are either faculties or functions. We hardly know what we mean by each of these terms and how they are related to each other. The important fact is, that we concern ourselves with helping the spirits of men to confront the universe with an awareness of their essential natures, as we discover them.

The world has said in many ways that we cannot have an honest horse race until we develop an honest human race. Yet the culture, religious and non-religious, has depended upon systems, rules, formats, laws, to improve the behavior of man. It seems that the church has often read right over such passages as John's Gospel when it says that the law (systems, rules, directives) came by Moses but grace and truth by Jesus Christ (John 1:17); or passages alleging that we are saved by grace not by works—outward, measurable action—but not "cheap grace" (Bonhoeffer) which overlooks the inherent challenge of God's call to freedom. Grace and faith which are genuine, issue in outward, measurable works but never originate in the visible world (compare Eph. 2 and James 2).

The church today needs to return to the Christian focus

on the core personality (heart) as the basic problem in living. It is a sad commentary on Christian scholarship that it has spent so much energy on archeology while its ministers have often had to learn about the soul from medical men and psychologists. One would think that if there is one thing which the church is an authority on it would be the spirits or souls or hearts (the interior functioning) of men. It can be said, I believe, that the church has repeatedly tried to get its mind on the souls of men. It is not uncommon for men and women of the church to find a peace and power which has saved them from formality, legalism, externality, and temporal addictions.

Precisely, what have Christian teachers meant by *salvation?* What are we saved from and what for? We are saved from compulsive, proud adherence to systems, laws, rules—from bigoted legalism; from egoistic, impulse ridden, chaotic behavior; from attitudes of hate, aloofness, destructiveness and indifference. We are saved for relatedness in joy and love; for free conduct which can afford to be left free because it has acknowledged its obligation; for adventure in growth, for spiritual pilgrimage, for the reach for maturity which knows no ceiling; for the kind of self-giving which is inspired by Christ and by the heroes of all time.

Salvation is God's taking us where we are and keeping us moving, with some regressions, of course, fairly steadily towards what we can become in *this* life—the next life is frequently the concern of those who are not doing a good job in this one. The true believer is growing in his confidence in and understanding of God! This makes him so assured of the reality of the Eternal that he does not fret over how he meets God or despair over his means of transportation in getting there. He simply acknowledges the mystery of death and accepts his confrontation by it with the faith that God knows what He is doing and that His will must be a good will.

All these matters are spiritual, interior, psychic. The church belongs enmeshed in such affairs. Psychology and psychiatry may be temporary intruders in this field or helpers to those who have missed the way of God. It will no doubt remain true for a long time to come, however, that religion is the psychiatry of the masses. Or better still, it is Christ, and not culture alone, which is able to put man together after science has analyzed him.

To be perfectly frank, I fear that I may have created false dilemmas in the way I have stated the above. God must be working for the health, maturity, integration, self-actualizing, and wholeness of all of His children—the recalcitrant and the obedient. Something is wrong with the understandings of man when psychiatry and religion, or science and theology, for that matter, become competitors instead of comrades. The distinction between the secular and the sacred is fading right before our eyes. This may be good. The needs of mankind are so great and so many-sided that those who are trying to meet those needs may well become colleagues.

Notice, for example, at how self-help groups have sprung up in this country. I refer to such organizations as Alcoholics Anonymous, Parents Without Partners, TOPS (Take Off Pounds Sensibly), Gamblers Anonymous, Recovery Incorporated. In 1962 there were catalogued 265 such groups.[2] This is a significant movement in our times. People in their loneliness and alienation band themselves together to help

[2]Cf. O. Hobart Mowrer, *The New Group Therapy* (Princeton, N.J.: Van Nostrand Company, Inc., 1964), p. IV, for further references and discussion along this line.

one another. Group therapy, America's distinctive contribution to modern psychology, has aided and abetted these movements, as well as contributing to its own insights. The fact is, people are helped or feel that they are. But all too often the church has stood off and looked askance at such organizations as Alcoholics Anonymous, as they have thrust themselves forward by the impetus of severe need.

The church itself is but a "congregation" or "assembly" (the literal meaning of the word) of people who have had a unique experience and reach for unique goals. The meeting church is the only church which has any reality. We may count names on a roster, noses in a sitting and listening pew, but the church consists of individuals who have renounced their individualism to become a part of the body of Christ. Members of a church are not only vis-à-vis, or eyeball to eyeball; they stand beside one another, back one another up, and look deep into one another's hearts. The church is a body (small or large) of people who have distinctive concerns and care for people in a unique manner.

Luke tried to put this spiritual Christian quality into words as he characterized the early church: "And all who believed were together and had all things in common . . . . And day by day, attending the temple together and breaking bread in their homes, they partook of food with glad and generous hearts" (Acts 2:44, 46). "Now the company of those who believed were of one heart and soul, and no one said that any of the things he possessed was his own, but they had everything in common" (Acts 4:32).

The modern threadbare word, "togetherness," hardly catches the depth of relationship of true Christians. There may be a kind of togetherness at the neighborhood tavern, or around the backyard swimming pool in suburbia, or even at the company cocktail party. The church must not forget that these are significant together experiences for large segments of our population; and to many church members even, these are much more meaningful than their church meetings.

James, in his *Letter* said, "You should get into the habit of admitting your sins to each other, and praying for each other, so that if sickness comes to you you may be healed" (5:16 Phillips). This is the way the early church perceived the church, as a "therapeutic community." Where do people confess their sins today? Most intimate sins and grievous faults are confessed to the professional therapist—pastoral counselor, psychiatrist, psychologist, or social worker. There is a reason why the church has been by-passed by the sick person who seeks salvation. The church must face this reason and repent of her failures.

I disagree strenuously with some of the ideas of the noted psychologist, O. Hobart Mowrer, especially in his attacks upon individual, one-to-one psychotherapy and in his endorsement of punishment as a restoring act.[3] Nevertheless, he has pointed his finger at the church for encouraging secretiveness, or for not emphasizing confessions, and he has

---

[3]It would seem that Mowrer has abandoned New Testament religion when he says: "Punishment is not basically a 'rejecting act', as is commonly assumed. It is rather, in its most legitimate form, a way of *restoring* the person to full status and fellowship, making him again acceptable and worthy of our cooperation and trust." (Ibid, p. 238). Does not punishment create fear and closedness? And who are we to say that a person is worthy of our trust only after he has been punished? Does either punishment or threat of punishment make people better motivated to behave? What of repentance? The Apostle John thought that fear and punishment were linked together, and that "perfect love casts our fear" (I John 4:18). One wonders if while we were bouncing legalism out the religious door, it has crept silently back through the psychological window.

See also William Klassen's criticism of Mowrer's misunderstanding of sin and forgiveness, *The Forgiving Community* (Philadelphia: The Westminster Press, 1966), pp. 218-219.

made a point which cannot help but receive our embarrassed acceptance. Dr. Mowrer puts it succinctly in a quotation from psychologist Sidney Jourard, with which he agrees: "Why, then, do we conceal instead of disclose? Loving is a scary business, because when you permit yourself to be known, you expose yourself not only to a lover's balm, but to a hater's bomb! He knows just where to plant them for maximum effect, when he knows you."[4]

The implications of Mowrer's and Jourard's emphasize on openness and disclosure has great possibilities for the church. God may be showing us something through group therapy, sensitivity groups, and the many self-help groups that are springing up in our midst.

To create the environment for confession, we must learn the true meaning of confidentiality. Certain professions such as medicine, law, and the ministry, talk about confidential communication. Some of these are reneging on this code of confidentiality on the grounds that their first loyalty is to the community. The important thing is to find out who can keep a confidence under all circumstances, except where life and health are in serious danger, and to include them in the Christian or professional fellowship. People will develop openness and honesty only in the presence of others who will guard confidences and who will not sit in judgment. The genius of such groups as Alcoholics Anonymous, Gamblers Anonymous, Parents Without Partners is that they accept their members with their distinctive problems and failures and try to find some other approach than guilt. They may be laymen and amateurs, but they take the individuals where

[4]*Ibid.*, p. 237. See also the very excellent work by Jourard, quoted here by Mowrer, *The Transparent Self* (D. Van Nostrand Company, Inc., 1964).

they are and receive their story in all of its sordidness. In short, they try to accept and understand and refuse to be judgmental.

What would happen to the church if it met in small communication groups and asked such soul searching questions as the following: When did I first get an impression about God—what He is like? Who first showed me tenderness or warmth? What are my deepest needs? How can I overcome the emotions of resentment and bitterness which so easily accumulates in us all? Who am I? What do I have a right to enjoy? How does God seem to me? What is prayer for? What are my sins? How can I best spend my life? How can I share my faith with others? I can imagine that each one of these questions, if faced with sincerity and transparency, could lead to employment of a whole talking session in most groups.

Those who are too closed (perhaps too proud) to enter into a self-revelation session would probably caricature this whole experience as an emotional or spiritual striptease. But how else are we to know one another? Jesus said to his disciples, "All that I have heard from my Father I have made known to you" (John 15:15).

Christian witnessing, a vague term, is but a form of self-revelation, or self-disclosure. The early Christians, when the culture tried to shut them up, said, "We cannot but speak of what we have seen and heard" (Acts 4:20). The good news of Christ is always a personal word about how we have experienced the Christian message. Exposition of the Scriptures without involvement in the personal commandment to me in my social situation is like giving the name, date, and circumstances of a great musical composition but being void of any aesthetic response to its performance.

The message of Christ to His disciples about their lack of wisdom has many applications to us. I have pointed out three: the failure to translate our ideas into everyday language; the importance of the church focusing on the inward aspects of religion; and the essentiality of relatedness as the climax of all religious striving.

It seems that Christ would say, "Get smart. The world's salesmen want to sell a perfume or a deodorant or enlist in a campaign. They have their own techniques. You want to bring individuals into a new and successful relationship with God and their fellow man. You want to help persons to become whole persons, to guide people in paths which they will feel are the highest and the best. If you really believe that Christ and His apostles had some unique secrets in this realm, find them. If your religion is dependent on a Person whom you believe is alive and knows how to make Himself known, get with it. Relate to Him. Let the church be the church, in the cathedral or in the market place. Let the Christian be a Christian, taking orders from the Living Christ!"

The late James Moffat said that in every congregation you will find a small group of believers surrounded by a larger group of those who believe that they believe. We are in a day when many seeming followers of our Lord do not even profess to believe in God. Yet they seem to be casting out demons in his name (see Mark 9:38-40). Perhaps they are not with us because we got sidetracked. Who knows? At least it behooves us to search our own hearts to see if we are open to whatever Word may be spoken to us. Those who believe that they believe become true believers the moment, and it the many moments, when they respond to Christ.

CHAPTER 11

Guts

My daughter, a senior at the University of Kansas, told me of a young Methodist pastor in their town of Lawrence who is able to speak to students. One Sunday I was free from speaking duties so I went to hear him at the eleven o'clock service. It was the third worship service of the morning for the Reverend Ronald Sunbye. I did not inquire whether the others were filled or not, but if I had not gotten there fifteen minutes early, I would not have been able to get that off-side seat near the back of the balcony.

The focus of the sermon centered around the theme of whether we ought to fall for that slogan which says that "charity begins at home." He was struggling with the issues both as a minister and as a living human being as a husband and a father. At the end he admitted that we really do not have the answers about how to love the world and, at the same time, love our families and friends. "There are no easy answers. We do not know at times whether to stay at home with the family or go out to those who seem to need us more. We really do not know. Yet we have to make decisions. We have to say yes or no; and do you know what it takes for you to come up with answers to such difficult questions? It takes guts!"

This is about the way he ended his sermon. Then he sat down. I could see why young people were coming to hear him. He was dealing with issues that we all face. And he was not afraid to use a word that we all use in private but ordinarily shun in the pulpit out of deference to the prudish members of the congregation. It is such a pity that religion has become nicey nice and prim and proper. Our elegant language often betrays our impotence and lack of spontaneity.

On a church-related college campus a few years ago, I heard a representative from the denominational headquarters say that people who use such words as "damn" and "hell" were showing that they did not have a good use of the English language and were "hurting their Christian testimony." Which was he worried about? Are the two equivalent? My response to the first is, "Whose English—the kings or the commoners?" To the second issue, Christian testimony, I would respond in good Bible language. "He that believeth not shall be damned" and "To hell with such a fragile testimony?" When being nice and using holy diction is equated with following Christ, I will take apple pie.

Recently I had lunch with a young minister who is experimenting with a new kind of communication, sermon dialogue in which the congregation responds by asking questions right in the middle of the "preached Word." Throughout the afternoon there were several small group discussions in the homes of various members. The sermon that day was on "Acceptance." In one of the homes a young man who was leading the discussion said, "What would some of you say if I told you that I, as a married man, have had three women on the side?" The discussion and the relative rise of blood pressures moved steadily up. In the process of talking about how faith applied to the workaday world and how the average man sees the church people he used a four-letter word—don't quibble about which one. The hostess called the pastor to say that this young man was not welcome in her home anymore. And the sermon had been on "Acceptance!" Perhaps the pastor should have preached on "Propriety."

Florence Allshorn of England has said: "I begin to think that guts comes next to love; anyway, love without them is a flimsy sentimental thing."[1] Our generation is trying to shake off the dust of Puritanism and find fresh, lively ways of talking about the facts of life. Courage would probably be as good a word for what we are talking about here if it were not for the fact that it has lost its lustre. It sounds archivish and museumish. After we dust it off we see that is means the same thing as gutty and guttish and "on the gut level." Slopping the hogs rings a bell with farmers. Administering to the swine is not the same thing. Likewise, intestinal fortitude is not the same as guts.

Now that we know what we are talking about, let's quit quibbling and examine the correlation between Christianity and courage. How needful is this quality in being the kind of genuine, gritty, gutty (sometimes grimy), glowing Christian who is called for today? How can a Christian convey courage in our casual, careless, convivial, corrupt, concealing, constipated world.

[1] J. H. Oldham, quoting Florence Allshorn, *Life Is Commitment* (New York: Harper and Row, Publishers Inc.), p. 50.

It is amazing how the early Christians conveyed courage. A typical remark about them is found in Acts 4:13: "Now when they saw the boldness of Peter and John, and perceived that they were uneducated, common men, they wondered; and they recognized that they had been with Jesus."

Paul in a delightful passage that likens our spiritual coping devices to a Roman soldier's armor says, "Therefore, take up God's armor; then you will be able to stand your ground when things are at their worst" (Ephesians 6:13, NEB). There you have it. The real test of religion, of maturity, of mental health, of spirituality is how we stand up when things are at their worst. Anyone can be religious or appear mature when he is in good health, when friends are loyal, when your insurance premiums are paid in advance, when the stock market is rising, when prospects of popularity and security are good. The test of maturity and of spirituality is when we are faced with disappointment, delay, or death.

Karle Wilson Baker has it right when he writes, in a poem called "Courage:"[2]

> Courage is armour
> A blind man wears;
> The calloused scar
> Of outlived despairs:
> Courage is Fear
> That has said its prayers.

I do not mind telling my close friends that I am scared to death. And I will probably die of fear. Millions have. I am scared of failure, of society, of the future, of the possibility

[2]Karle Wilson Baker, "Courage" from *Masterpieces of Religious Verse*, Ed. by James D. Morrison, Reprinted by permission of Harper and Row, Publishers. Permission granted by Rev. Charles L. Wallis, Keuka College, Keuka Park, N. Y.

of the dropping of an atomic bomb, of rejection by my friends and contamination by my enemies. I fear disease, despair, dispiritedness, and death. However, I hope that I will not turn tail and run. Many a suicide has done just that. It is much easier to run behind the barricades of tradition and conformism than it is to march out onto the field of battle and challenge our enemies to the jousts of our new day.

To be more specific, where are guts most needed in the last half of the twentieth century? Three times in this chapter the word "death" has appeared as one of the objects that calls for guts. This may be man's major fear as many modern theologians and psychiatrists say. I doubt it. This does not mean that I do not have a healthy respect for death. A part of the time I face "the grim reaper;" the remainder of the time I face away from him and act like I am not time-bound. Nevertheless, we all know "that death, a necessary end, will come when it will come."

I find my mind secretly going back to Pascal's famous paragraph which depicts our human situation:

> Let us imagine a number of men in chains, and all condemned to death, where some are killed each day in the sight of the others, and those who remain see their own fate in that of their fellows, and wait their turn, looking at each other sorrowfully and without hope. It is an image of the condition of man.[3]

This speaks to me more than all of the research of modern psychologists, even the existentialists.[4]

[3]*Pascal's Pensees* (New York: E. P. Dutton and Co., Inc.), p. 60, number 199.
[4]Cf. Herman Feifel, *The Meaning of Death* (New York: McGraw-Hill, 1959).

Laotzu spoke what many have responded to, in two separate passages:

> A man with outward courage dares to die
> A man with inward courage dares to live. . .
> . . . .
> Death is no threat to people
> Who are not afraid to die.[5]

The problem in the second quotation lives in the fact that modern man, with increased awareness of the mysterious and powerful unconscious, suspects that though he may not be conscious of any death-fear, he may be living his whole life trying to ward off the inevitable hour. Laotzu was certainly right in his emphasis on the kind of courage which dares to live. Here, it would seem, is where most of us prove ourselves to be gutless wonders.

All of us have trembled in our boots over the sound of an explosion, or the scream of a fire siren, or the look on our physician's face, or the knowing look of our enemy, or "a close call" on the highway. Most of these upsets can be handled by a couple of tranquilizers or a good shot of whiskey. At least, these are the ways that a good percent of our culture handle such fears. It may be well argued that both tranquillizers and alcohol are courage substitutes. If they were used in temporary upsets only, the case against them would be weak.

Our deepest and most crippling fears are not death nor near death reactions, but nagging, gnawing fears that do not relate to one event or episode. It takes guts to live with masked and subtle fears which, like the poor, are always with us. I refer to such fears as accompany the terror of being in error, the risk of being wrong, the animosities of our enemies, and the menace of meaninglessness.

Error and truth, for practical purposes, are opposites. It may not seem terrifying to some to be in error but for some of us who are encapsulated in a pride system, to be caught red-handed with an error that is so obvious that even a child should have known better, simply fractures us.

Who has not flunked an exam, or run a red light because of inadvertance, or given someone directions to a street only to remember later that we were in error? It takes guts to enroll in some courses which we know to be extraordinarily difficult. Only the brave can face a whole stack in a library and stay long enough to research a problem. Or who can take arms against a sea of human myths and superstitions without feeling that our few strokes will hardly make a wave's difference in the flood which rushes over us? So we succumb to cynicisms. After all, who will be influenced by our few gestures of pointing the way toward the true path?

It takes all kinds of courage to take ourselves in hand and try to search out some little corner of truth knowing that what we find may be either a complete error or a half truth, or such an infinitesmal bit of insight that others can hardly notice it. It must be this kind of limitedness which makes us grab ahold of slovenly slogans and delude ourselves with deadly dogmas. Two anonymous quotations come to mind: "Three percent of the people think; twelve percent think that they think, the other eighty-five per cent look for a slogan;" And, "a man's best friend is his *dogma.*" It is so much safer, and twice as comfortable, to live by slogans and dogmas. The possibility of error often strikes terror to our careful minds.

A second area of living which taxes our inner strength is the risk of being wrong in conduct. Maybe, even, the risk of being bad. Risky living is as anxiety creating as adventurous thinking. Both involve the rising up to look at the alternative roads which we may take; then, with our hat in hand move out to pursue a course of thinking, or of action. Both are acts. To act rather than merely to react, or rather than to entrench ourselves behind pat answers or beaten paths—this takes guts.

Man is a decision maker. Herein lies his glory and his shame. In Eden it was his downfall. In Gethsemane and on Golgotha decisions within the respective spheres of small freedom were marks of heroism. What else could Jesus have done in Gethsemane and on Golgotha? We often ask such silly questions, as if man is ever in a spot where he has no alternatives. But to answer the question about Jesus in His crises: He could have became embittered and rebellious. Somehow He found the words in Gethsemane—"Not my will but thine be done"—which kept His face toward His destiny. On the cross His seven sayings showed that He was still in charge of Himself. He convinced the reporters and the Gospel writers that He laid life down "of his own accord."

A senior college girl was being pressed by her boy friend to get married. Her life had been complicated by a domineering mother, a culture that is confused about sex, and a religion which had not made a clear transition from legalism to risk living by the principles of love and justice. Her reply to him was: 'I am not ready to get married—not until I can claim my life for myself." Her point was a good one. Until an individual can claim his life for himself he is in no position to claim selfhood, to resist the tyrannies all about him, or even to give himself to God. The Prodigal Son made a very gutty—though foolish—move when he demanded of his father his part of the family estate. Later it took even more guts to look at the overall picture, "when he came to himself," and make a clean-cut decision to go back home.

Sin or saintliness (who wants it?) both take nerve. Whatever course we pursue may be wrong. This is not to say that one road is as good as another. Such a generalization may be as arrogant as Puritanism or Communism. The point is, we do not know when we are right or when we are wrong in many instances. We are as doomed to uncertainty, to finitude, to walking by some kind of faith as a hunter who is lost in a foggy woods and must trust his sense of direction. Perhaps the above figure is overdrawn. Let us say, then, that many times in life we are faced with the painful fact that we have to make decisions about morals, vocation, business, marriage, money, friendships, and a thousand other things when all of the evidence points to the fact that we may be wrong. To keep on acting, making decisions, risking failure, living in uncertainty, flying by the seat of our pants, moving from within—this is the essence of gutty living.

One of the crippling factors in courageous thinking or risky decisions is the ever present possibility of rejection by our fellow human beings. I do not refer merely to refutation or disagreement or even some back-turning from those about us. A certain amount of this is a part of every life.

The enslavement to public opinion, the controlling force of the collective will, the bondage to mass media influences— these are factors which call for discrimination and choices which puzzle and paralyze modern man. It is not so much that we have what Karen Horney called "the tyranny of the should": it is a question of which *should* or *ought* we allow to speak to us. Herein lies the heart of our moral problems.

We obviously cannot go it alone and to go off into our

little world of imagination or to create our own system of behavior is hardly realistic. Only the psychotic can afford that luxury, and he ends up having to be restrained. "None of us lives to himself, and none of us dies to himself" (Rom. 14:7).

Conscience is a kind of "knowing-with" others as any dictionary will show. This does not come to the heart of the problem though as I suggested above. The question is, Which others? The hippies or the squares? The Christians or the Muslims? The Communists or the capitalists? We once had only the choices afforded by a small community, next of a pluralistic culture, now of a multi-pluralistic world. Who knows what new choices we may find out in space? Of course, one human mind can consider or attend to only a certain number of demands or calls, but these have increased at such a speed with the mass media of TV and radio that today the backwoodsman, even, has to make up his mind about what he thinks about LSD and topless waitresses.

The practical aspects of the problems of choice in the face of what people will think of us, however, arise where they have for centuries, over such simple matters as what we shall spend our money for (or who give it to), what is the best use of our time, how shall we treat the members of our families, to whom shall we be open, and what shall we consider important.

It is in confronting these stimulus-imputs (to resort to current social psychology jargon) that we find ourselves experiencing both guilt and shame. Guilt is oriented toward God and our internalized figures—this is largely what we call conscience. We feel guilty when we have let God or ourselves down, as we perceive the situation. Shame, on the other hand, is related more to "significant others." "What will they think?" is the important question. If there is a chance of them laughing at us, throwing rocks at us, or not even speaking to us, we will experience shame or its cover-up, anger.

When we experience some kind of rejection, in other words, our self-image is shaken and unless we can find an instant rationale we lose face. If we let ourselves down, or if we are rejected by our fellowman, in either case, something happens to us inside. We say, "We lose heart," or "We feel guilty," or "We hate ourselves." Often it is hard to distinguish between shame and guilt. When we begin to reason about what we are experiencing, at that point, courage becomes a prime ingredient.

It takes guts to stand up against those with whom we have stood and say as Martin Luther did, "Here I stand; I can do no other." It took courage for Adam and Eve to even answer God's query, "Where art thou?" The courage to respond to those who call to us, the guts to try for a deep, open, warm relationship, in spite of our failure—this takes more nerve at times than it does to tell someone off. The go-to-hell attitude of many people is nothing more than a defense against relatedness. Similarly, the "I'm-right-and-you're-wrong" approach to conflict situations precludes the possibility of being found wrong. Perhaps it is not an exaggeration to say that much of the superficiality of our living is because we are afraid to reveal ourselves to each other. We are afraid of losing face, and then of losing heart. We stop to think too often and too tendermindedly. Perhaps it would be more accurate to say that we think too defensively.

> Thus conscience does make cowards of us all;
> And thus the native hue of resolution
> Is sicklied o'er with the pale cast of thought.
> Shakespeare, *Hamlet,* III, I

It is when we stop to think of the feelings that others will have toward us that we decide to remain as we are. We may be disgraced if we act. Even if history were to exonerate us we could not stand the evil eye of those who would criticize us. Paul Tournier talks of the incredible tenacity of feelings of guilt and shame even when they are unfounded in a chapter entitled "Judgment is Destructive."

> But in all fields, even those of culture and art, other people's judgment exercises a paralyzing effect. Fear of criticism kills spontaneity; it prevents men from showing themselves and expressing themselves freely, as they are. Much courage is needed to paint a picture, to write a book, to erect a building designed along new architectural lines, or to formulate an independent opinion or an original idea.[6]

We face, then, two pertinent questions to put to the proclaimers of grace. Can grace overcome disgrace? Which is stronger, once a man has achieved the maturity to look at himself, guilt or grace? If grace does not give us guts to face disgrace even if we go to what Camus called "the hell of history," we cannot have real character. And if guilt, our inner selfscolding, cannot be faced with fortitude, sooner or later we will be slain by either hypocrisy or suicide.

The late Paul Tillich suggests the way out when he defined courage as the ability "to accept oneself as accepted in spite of being unacceptable." He says further:

> Here, however, is the point where the religious "acceptance as being accepted" transcends medical healing . . . The acceptance by God, his forgiving or justifying act, is the

[6]Paul Tournier, *Guilt and Grace* (Harper & Row, Publishers, 1962), p. 98.

only and ultimate source of a courage to be which is able
to take the anxiety of guilt and condemnation into itself.[7]

The climax of gutty living is to find meaning in life when
what we thought meant something goes up in smoke. The
difference between people is partly in their reactions to life
when their foundations have been shaken. "My bridges are
washed out," a man said to me. "What I thought was a road
ahead has become a dead-end street. There is no hope. What
do you do when you do not know what to do?" This speech
left me speechless. I dared not become one of Job's com-
forters.

There are times when the band stops playing and the
parade stops dead in its tracks and for a few moments, sometimes days, we shudder and wait to see if the lights are going
completely out. In such times we must "stand"—as we quoted
Paul in the first of this chapter, "to stand your ground when
things are at their worst." At such times we say with Alfie,
"What is it all about?" Meaning goes out the window when
trouble knocks hard enough at the door.

Finding meaning in life usually, however, is not a matter
of standing tragedy or of answering ambiguity. The tragic
and the ambiguous fracture us, partly because we are so
set on knowing good and evil. We want to know what God
knows. I am not arguing for a blind faith or for an unin-
formed strapping down of our drive for knowledge. It would
seem, however, that we might as well accept the fact that
we walk in some kind of faith (meeting with and depend-
ence upon revelation) or we walk in darkness.

The gutty quests of man, it should be admitted at this

[7]Paul Tillich, *The Courage to Be* (New Haven: Yale University Press,
1952), p. 166.

point, are not for nerve to stand the enervating, but for something which will make our little lives stand out. We all respond to something which grabs us, turns us on, makes our eyes glisten, space-walks us. Some people are satisfied to live along like the turning of a water wheel in a stream until some part of the machinery breaks down; and then, die and fade away.

It takes an inner creative thrust to reach out to that which space-walks us, to repeat a figure. Perhaps that is why LSD, marijuana, mescaline, and alcohol are becoming so much a part of our culture. It takes courage to take an LSD trip, I would suppose. At the moment I am too concerned for my own sanity to risk it.

Paul makes an interesting comment: "Do not give way to drunkenness and the dissipation that goes with it, but let the Holy Spirit fill you" (Eph. 5:18, NEB). Alcoholic beverages were the nearest thing to psychedelic drugs available in Bible lands and times. It is strange that Paul should have associated wine with being filled with the Spirit. Both affect the moods. Both remove some inhibitory and rational controls and allow some spontaneous aspects of the human personality to come forward. When we are filled with the Spirit, as anyone who reads the *Acts of the Apostles* can see, we become "inner directed" and have a boldness which overcomes reticence and fear. We move out of ruts and away from closures into new ways of joyous living.

The life of faith is one of adventure, uncharted action, creative planning, courageous conquests. It is what Kierkegaard describes as "the knight of faith," of infinite resignation, who "lives as carefree as a ne'er-do-well, and yet he buys up the acceptable time at the dearest price, for he does not do the least thing except by virtue of the absurd . . . Most people live dejectedly in worldly sorrow and joy; they are the ones who sit along the wall and do not join in the dance. The knights of infinity are dancers and possess elevation."[8]

This reminds me of the words of Moses to the slaves who were about to enter the land of Canaan: "I call heaven and earth to witness this day against you, that I have set before you life and death, blessing and cursing, therefore choose life"! (Deut. 30:19). This seems to me to be the picture of mankind before God, 1500 B.C. or probably in A.D. 2000: we are faced with blessing or cursing, life or death. The trouble seems to be that we do not have the courage to choose life.

How is all of this tied in with finding meaning in life? What are "for instances?" A young lady from a status-ridden home repudiated her relatives' dreams and hopes for her and took a degree in social work in order to do what she wanted to do with her life. A young man refused a partnership with his wealthy father and became an artist, turning down ease and plenty, but finding self-fulfillment and peace of mind. A husband gets up and goes to church in spite of the fact that his wife thinks it is silly. Children see the barrenness of their parents' lives and turn to religious faith which their parents think is superstition. A girl pregnant out of wedlock by a boy whom she may not love decides to adopt the baby out rather than marry the man and get a divorce later as her family would prefer.

"Profiles of courage" could be drawn from the files of most families. Alongside them, however, would be the records of cowardly retreats, passed-up opportunities, unespoused

[8] *A Kirkegaard Anthology,* ed. by Robert Bretall (Princeton: University Press, 1946), pp. 120-121.

causes which set history back, and Judas-like betrayals which marred the scutcheon of an otherwise admirable life.

The crux of the courageous life is to be found, not simply in non-conformism, but in the decisions that we make from within which give us the feeling of genuineness. This is why counselors, parents, teachers, pastors, and any others in the helping professions, cannot make decisions for us. If they do, they take away our authenticity. They may helpfully increase our understanding of ourselves and our grasp or reality. Only *we* know our interior life, and only *we* can draw from within us that answer to life's calls which will give a feeling that "This is what I wish to do and I will do it."

It is at this point that guts and grace unite. When Paul wrote, "All who are led by the Spirit of God are the sons of God . . . it is the Spirit himself bearing witness with our spirit that we are the children of God" (Rom. 8:14, 16), he was reaching up to the zenith of authentic living. It takes nerve to rely on the in-the-moment leadership of the Divine within us and beyond us, and even with fear and trembling, move forward or stand still.

If this seems illusory or delusional to many, they must find their own way of living. The Christian does not blush when he talks of the risk of faith or walking in the Spirit because he has already acknowledged that he is a dependent creature —dependent on grace—and from this he has the gall to move forward not knowing where he is going. The feeling of satisfaction and meaning is its own verification of the value of his position. He feels that the life of courage is the only one worth living and that, fail as he does at times or stumble blindly and thoughtlessly as he does at other times, he must have the heart to stand—to stand up and be counted—and to march forward on the legs of faith.